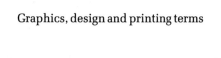
Graphics, design and printing terms

By the same author

Graphics handbook, 1966
Illustrated graphics glossary, 1980

Ken Garland

Graphics, design and printing terms

An international dictionary

Design Press

First U.S. edition, First Printing

Copyright © 1980, 1989 by Ken Garland
Printed in the United States of America
Designed by Ken Garland and Associates
Typeset by Nene Photypesetters
in Linotron 202 9/10½ pt. Melior

Library of Congress Cataloging-in-Publication Data
Garland, Ken.

   Graphics, design, and printing terms : an international dictionary
 / Ken Garland.
      p.   cm.
      ISBN 0-8306-3448-7
      1. Computer graphics—Dictionaries.   2. Printing, Practical-
-Dictionaries.   I. Title.
   T385.G37   1990
   006.6′03—dc20   89-38697
                                                                    CIP

248p. : ill. ; 23 cm.

Thanks

to Harriet Cowder and Josef Gross for their photographic contribu-
tions; to Colin Bailey, Peter Cole and Paul Cleal for their diligent
work on the drawn illustrations and the layout;
to my wife, Wanda, for her patience and encouragement;
and to all those of my colleagues and students who have helped me in
the quest for definitions that are precise enough to satisfy the pedant
yet plain enough to inform the beginner.

Dedicated

to the fond memory of the late Bob Chapman, who was first of all my
student, then my associate and friend, in the hope that some of his
fine passion for clarity in the business of communication may have
been transmitted through me to this work and thence to its readers.

Introduction

This last decade has seen the much-heralded explosion of information technology. In its wake we have found ourselves wallowing in a morass of jargon. Glossaries and dictionaries of technology now abound in the fields of photocomposition, word-processing, computer-aided design and computer usage generally. Unfortunately, there is a tendency for contradictions to abound also, between one dictionary and another.

Glossarians are not helped by the vagaries of equipment manufacturers. For example, the traditional Anglo-American pica em is properly defined as 0.66604in – approximately, but by no means exactly, one-sixth of an inch – by all typographic authorities. The IBM company, however, with all the assumed authority of a powerful multi-national, decided to tidy up this unsatisfactory situation and proclaimed the pica (or at any rate their pica) as being exactly one-sixth of an inch, or 0.6666...in. So now we have two conflicting definitions and the consequent confusion that arises if one is mistakenly substituted for the other. When this sort of mistake is compounded by its inclusion in a dictionary of terms, one would be forgiven for despairing of such would-be authorities.

Aye, there's the rub. It is precisely those terms imported from some other technology than our own that we stumble over most frequently, to our own embarrassment and others' scorn: they are the ones we go to dictionaries for, and it would be a downright disservice to those of us who have to call on a wide number of skills in our work, if the compilers of specialist dictionaries retreated into their own professional or technological enclaves, merely reinforcing their exclusiveness. How to avoid the kind of confusions presented by the IBM 'pica'? Ah, if only we could ignore these treacherous picas and settle for the indisputable millimetre, but it is either too late or too soon to insist on universal standards; still less feasible to propose the elimination of the many synonyms that cluster round many of our craft and technical terms. In any case, are these not an adornment to the language rather than a nuisance? It was pure delight, for example, to uncover seven synonyms for 'exclamation mark': astonisher, bang, shriek, squealer, striker, screamer and – most delightful of all – dog's cock. The day when we are to be allowed only one word for one thing will be a sad day indeed.

No, there is only one answer to the question of how one can prepare a dictionary of terms that spans several fields of skill and technology: with very great care, and with the benefit of much good advice from colleagues (even if some of it is at first sight contradictory). In the process of sifting, sorting and selection for this work, there may well be gaps, even a few solecisms or infelicities. If so, readers are urged to write to the author, care of the publisher, and let him know, so that additions or amendments may be included in any new edition.

Finally, a message to those of you who are just venturing into a new area of technology and are alarmed at your unfamiliarity with the jargon that is being bandied about by apparent experts: take heart, it is very probable that many of them are not too sure what the jargon means either, and never had the nerve to ask a colleague for a clear definition of a term that had been handed to them as part of some magic rite. Again, those who *do* know the meaning of a jargon word may hug it to themselves for devious reasons connected with status. Don't let them get away with it: any technical term that cannot be explained in words comprehensible to the intelligent lay person is best relegated to the vast scrapyard of unnecessary nonsense language that litters every technology. Whatever you do, don't use a term you don't understand, just to keep in with the others; that's a fool's game if ever there was one.

Note: single quotes in the text indicate a cross-reference; when such an item is followed by an arrow the reader is specially recommended to consult that entry.

A

AA — initials of *a*uthor's *a*lteration : indication on proof that cost of type correction is author's or publisher's responsibility (used in US but not common in UK)

AAAA — initials of *A*merican *A*ssociation of *A*dvertising *A*gencies

AAP — initials of *A*ssociation of *A*merican *P*ublishers

ABA — initials of *A*merican *B*ooksellers *A*ssociation

A, B and C series of paper sizes — triple range of paper sizes originally established as 'DIN' standards, then adopted by International Standards Organization (ISO), of which 'A' Series is intended for all kinds of stationery and printed matter, 'B' Series as intermediate alternatives and 'C' Series for envelopes; all sizes are as trimmed or made up and are given in millimetres:

A0 1189 × 841	B0 1414 × 1000	C0 1297 × 917
A1 841 × 594	B1 1000 × 707	C1 917 × 648
A2 594 × 420	B2 707 × 500	C2 648 × 458
A3 420 × 297	B3 500 × 353	C3 458 × 324
A4 297 × 210	B4 353 × 250	C4 324 × 229
A5 210 × 148	B5 250 × 176	C5 229 × 162
A6 148 × 105	B6 176 × 125	C6 162 × 114
A7 105 × 74	B7 125 × 88	C7 114 × 81
A8 74 × 52	B8 88 × 62	specials:
A9 52 × 37	B9 64 × 44	DL 220 × 110
A10 37 × 26	B10 44 × 31	C7/6 162 × 81

all sizes are proportionate reductions of basic 0 sheet, sides being in ratio $1 : \sqrt{2}$ (1 : 1.4142):

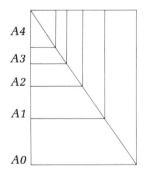
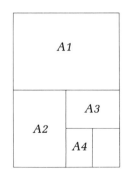

A0 = one square metre
untrimmed sheet size for unbled work: RA0 1220 × 860mm
untrimmed sheet size for bled work: SRA0 1280 × 900mm
DL envelopes are specially intended to accommodate A4 sheets folded twice to ⅓A4

8

above the fold	newspaper term for top half of paper above horizon fold
abscissa	co-ordinate running parallel to *x*-axis in 'coordinate graph' →
abstract (as noun)	summary of book, periodical feature, report or learned paper
a/c	account mark, used on invoices, statements, etc; stands for '*a*ccount *c*urrent'
accented/diacritical signs	those commonly used in European languages are:

å	boll	ç	cedilla	č š ř	haček
è	grave	ô	circumflex	ø	bar
é	acute	ñ	tilde	ä ö ü	umlaut

in addition, diaeresis (¨) is used in English to denote second of two adjacent vowels which is to be pronounced separately, as in 'naïve'

access (as verb) (computers)	process of obtaining data from computer
access time (computers)	time taken to locate and 'read' item of data from computer
accessing (computers)	retrieving data from computer 'store'; access time is key factor in measuring relative efficiency of computer
accordion fold	method of folding paper in which each fold is in opposite direction to previous one (see 'folding methods')
accuracy aid (computer graphics)	pre-programmed function permitting precise positioning on 'interactive display' →
acetate-based material	see 'tracing materials'
achromatic colour correction	in colour reproduction, method of filtering out unnecessary depth of primary colours down to minimum effective amounts of each; may be used to achieve economy in running time or cost of ink
acoustic coupler (computers)	cheap form of 'modem' →
acronym	set of letters formed from initial letters of words in phrase, and of other letters in words if needed, to compose a pronounceable (hence memorable) 'word', eg: ICOGRADA for *I*nternational *C*ouncil of *G*raphic *D*esign *A*ssociations
across the gutter	in book or periodical, any matter that prints across back margins; usually said of photograph extending over both pages of 'double spread' →
ADC (computers)	initials of *a*nalog to *d*igital *c*onversion

addendum
(pl: addenda)

Latin for 'thing to be added'; used to denote item or items added subsequently to text of book

additive colour mixing

reproducing colours by mixing lights, as distinct from 'subtractive colour mixing' →:

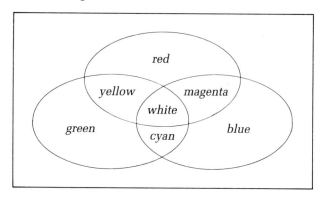

address (computers)

character or group of characters employed to identify location in 'memory' → of computer

address space
(computer graphics)

area of screen that can be identified by coordinate system

addressable point
(computer graphics)

position on screen that can be identified by coordinate system

Adherography

trade name for duplicating process in which image is formed by adherence of powder (toner) to sticky, latent image

adhesive binding

one in which 'sections/signatures' → are cut off at back and leaves so formed are secured by adhesive without sewing (see also 'perfect binding')

adjustable set-square/triangle

drawing implement which pivots at one corner, calibrated to provide desired angle of inclination:

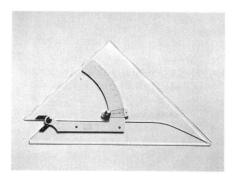

ADP	1) initials of *a*dvanced *d*ata *p*rocessing 2) initials of *a*utomatic *d*ata *p*rocessing
advanced copies	limited quantity of new publication made up in advance of main quantity for publicity, promotion or review purposes
agate line	unit of measurement used in US newspaper advertising to denote column depth (14 agate lines = 1 inch); derived from traditional name for 5½pt type
AGI	initials of *A*lliance *G*raphique *I*nternationale : world-wide clique of well-known graphic designers and illustrators who gather together from time to time for purpose of mutual admiration
AIGA	initials of *A*merican *I*nstitute of *G*raphic *A*rts, founded in 1914 in New York to 'do all things which would raise the standard and the extension and development towards perfection of the graphic arts in the US'
aiming symbol (computers)	synonym for 'cursor' →
airbrush	pressure gun with very fine nozzle, used for graded tone effects in artwork, especially retouching of photographs
ALA	initials of *A*merican *L*ibrary *A*ssociation
albertype	early name for 'collotype' →, after Joseph Albert, who pioneered the process
albumen plate	lithographic plate made from photographic negative using light-sensitive coating, formerly containing white of egg (albumen); also known as 'surface plate' as distinct from 'deep-etch plate' →
ALGOL	see 'computer languages'
algorithmics	study of problem solving by use of predetermined sets of procedural instructions, as distinct from 'heuristics' →; 'algorithm' is one set of fixed instructions for carrying out process, and may be either 'ordinary language algorithm' or 'computer algorithm'
aliasing (computer graphics)	irregular effect apparent in graphics display, where curves and diagonals are imperfectly rendered by rectilinear scanning pattern; also known as 'jaggies':

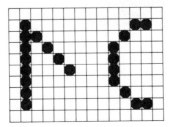

aligning numerals	synonym for 'lining figures/numerals' →
alignment	lining up type or other graphic matter to common horizontal or vertical line (but see also 'ranged'); sometimes spelled 'alinement'
alignment chart	same as 'nomogram' →
all-in-hand	state of typesetting job after all copy has been passed out to compositors
all-up	state of print job after all copy has been set
alphabet length	measurement, in points or picas, of width of lower-case alphabet of given typeface and size, set to 'normal' or 'standard' character spacing:

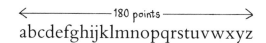

alphageometric (computer graphics)	in 'videotex' → system, graphic display on screen of linear figures and filling-in of these, as well as alphanumeric display:

alphamosaic (computer graphics)	in 'videotex' → system, method of composing simple, rather crude pictures or letters on screen by means of mosaic of 3 × 2 rectangles; no use for curves or diagonals:

alphanumeric set	strictly speaking, set of alphabetic letters and numerals, but may also be stretched to include other signs, such as + =
ALU (computers)	initials of *arithmetic and logic unit*: device that performs such functions in 'central processor unit' →

ambient light that which results in illumination of scene from all directions

AMFIS acronym for *A*utomatic *M*icrofilm *I*nformation *S*ystem

ammonia duplication process form of 'diazo' → process in which latent image is made visible by exposure to evaporating ammonia

ampersand symbol for 'and' derived from fusion of letters in Latin word *et*:

     &   &   &   &   &   &   &   &   &   &   &

selection of ampersands

anaglyph composite stereoscopic picture printed in superimposed, complementary colours for viewing through special coloured spectacles

analog computer one devised to represent variables in problems and to construct conceptual models (analogs) of them; note that alternate spelling 'analogue' is not now used in this context

analog dial traditional form of dial, eg: clockface in which position of hands is analogy of time of day represented; as contrasted with 'digital dial':

Anchor acronym for *A*lpha-*N*umeric *Ch*aracter Generat*or*: facility developed in early 1970s by British Broadcasting Corporation for keying in alphanumerics on television as fast as they can be typed

angles (geometric) types of angles are:

acute angle: *right angle:* *obtuse angle:* *reflex angle:*
less than 90° *90°* *more than 90°* *more than 180°*

aniline ink one made from coal-tar, commonly used in 'flexography' →

animatics simply made, usually repetitive, animated film or video sequence of short duration; sometimes employed to substitute temporarily for more elaborate animation

animation representation of motion by sequential photography of series of images on cinefilm or videotape; may be computer-generated

13

animation stand another name for 'rostrum' →; more common in US

ANSI initials of American National Standards Institute

answer print in cinefilm, first projection print of new film, submitted to film maker by process lab before more copies are made; also known as 'approval print'

anti-aliasing
(computer graphics) using techniques such as overlapping 'picture elements' → or varying their intensity so as to reduce jagged effect of 'aliasing' →:

0	0	0	0	0	0	0	0	0	0	0
0	3	3	3	3	0	0	0	0	0	0
0	3	3	3	3	2	0	0	0	0	0
0	3	3	3	3	3	1	0	0	0	0
0	3	3	3	3	3	3	0	0	0	0
0	3	3	3	3	3	3	2	0	0	0
0	3	3	3	3	3	3	3	1	0	0
0	3	3	3	2	3	3	3	3	0	0
0	3	3	3	2	2	3	3	3	2	0
0	3	3	3	2	0	3	3	3	3	1
0	3	3	3	2	0	1	3	3	3	3

pixel intensity levels 0, 1, 2, 3

anti-set-off spray one that may be applied to newly printed sheet so as to prevent 'set-off' →

Antiope name of character/graphics code for French 'videotex' system (see also 'Didon')

Antiqua German term denoting 'roman type' as distinct from 'black letter'

antique paper unsized, or lightly sized, material with rough, matt finish, usually bulky; used mainly for books

aperture
(of camera lens) opening of lens of camera, varied in diameter (unless fixed) by means of diaphragm (iris); size of aperture is indicated by '*f*- number', often called '*f* stop' and is one factor in calculating exposure time:

fully open at f2.8   stopped down to f5.6   stopped down to f11

aperture card one having inset frame or frames for filing and viewing 'microfilm' →

aphysical office
(computers) one that is not so much a place to work in as network to which people 'tap-in'; sometimes referred to as 'office-of-the-future'

API	initials of *American Paper Institute*
appearing size	optical size of type as against its nominated point size; typefaces of same nominated type size may have different appearing sizes:

abcdefghijklmnopqrst   abcdefghijklmnopqrst
12pt Bembo   *12pt Plantin*

appendix (pl: appendices)	part of 'end-matter' → of book, usually for purpose of enlarging on some element in text or to give supporting statistics
applications software (computers)	that which is intended for specific purpose and so is not suitable for general computer tasks
apron	extra paper on outer edge of leaf forming 'fold-out' →; term more common in US
arabesque	type of 'printer's flower' →
arabic numerals	symbols 1 2 3 4 5 6 7 8 9 0 as distinct from roman numerals; more properly 'hindu-arabic numerals', since they orginated in India around 500AD, were adopted by Arabs about AD900 and Spanish by AD1000:

hindu numerals

arabic numerals

archival paper	one with specially durable properties, particularly in relation to acidic change and colour fading
archiving (computers)	offline storing of data, usually on 'floppy disk' →, 'rigid disk' → or 'magnetic tape' →
area composition	in photocomposition, operation of setting made-up pages in varying formats for advertisements, tables, pages of periodicals and the like, following arrangement of these by use of 'video layout system' →
area search (computers)	examination of large area of 'file' → to select general category for further scrutiny
array	ordered arrangement, as in tabular display
art	may be used as abbreviation for 'artwork' →, especially in US, where it does not imply completeness
art paper	synonym for 'coated paper' → more common in UK than US
artificial intelligence (computers)	ability of some computers to perform operations resembling human capacity to learn and make decisions

artwork	any matter prepared for photomechanical reproduction; known in US as 'mechanical' → if complete
arty-farty	client's term for graphic design which is imaginative and innovatory
ASA	initials of *American Standards Association*; when prefixed to a number shown on film stock, it denotes relative 'film speed' → for calculating exposure
asap, ASAP	initials of '*as soon as possible*'; rather pointless phrase often appended to orders for photography, processing, print, etc
ascender	that part of certain lower-case letters, such as b, d, f, h, appearing above the 'x-height' →
ascender line	imaginary horizontal line connecting tops of ascender letters, often (but not necessarily) corresponding to 'cap line' →:

cap line   ascender line

Bembo

ASCII, ASCii (pron: askey)	acronym for *American Standard Code for Information Interchange*; most widely used character code for use in computers, using standard eight bit 'byte' → to represent 128 possible character combinations
ASID	initials of *American Society of Industrial Designers*
ASIS	initials of *American Society for Information Science*
aspect ratio	in cinefilm and TV, ratio of frame height to frame width: in 35mm cinefilm it is 3.155 : 4.34; in 16mm cinefilm, 2.94 : 4.10; and in TV, 3 : 4
ASPIC (computers)	acronym for *Author's Pre-programmed Interfacing Codes*, used in UK to specify commands to computer
assembly	generic term covering activity of putting together components of artwork, typesetting reproduction proofs, etc
asterisk	type character used as first order of 'reference marks' → for footnotes; also used on occasion for unprintable words like f * * *
astonisher	printer's slang for exclamation mark (more common in US)
ATypI	acronym for *Association Typographique Internationale*, founded in 1957 'to bring about a better understanding of typography, a higher level of typographic design, and to secure international protection for typefaces'
augustijn	12pt typographic unit of measurement in use in Netherlands,

16

identical to 'cicero' in France and Germany →; called '*aug*' for short

author's correction
any correction, deletion or addition to proof which is not result of printer's error; known as 'author's alteration' in US (see 'AA')

author's proof
one supplied to customer by printer, usually containing corrections from 'printer's reader' →

auto-kerning
in photocomposition, automatic implementation of pre-programmed 'kerning pairs' →

autolithography
process of drawing directly onto lithographic stone or plate without use of photography

automatic proofreading
somewhat misleading term applied to provision in some text-handling systems for correcting words that are commonly or consistently misspelt

automatic transfer press
'web-fed' → machine on which successive print jobs are run without pause for change over

autopaster
device on 'web-fed' → press that secures fresh web (reel) of paper without need to stop machine; also known as 'flying paster'

autopositive
photographic material or process which provides positive image of original without intervening negative stage

autoreversal film
one used to make positive image from positive, or negative image from negative, without need for intermediate stage

AVA
initials of *audio-visual aids* : woolly portmanteau term covering slide and film strip projectors, overhead projectors, closed-circuit TV and tape recorders, whether sound-vision linked or not

a/w, A/W
abbreviation for 'artwork' →

axonometric projections
'orthographic projections' → in which object is inclined in relation to picture plane, as distinct from 'multiview projections'; there are three forms:

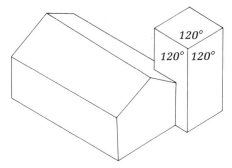

isometric projection: all three axes of rectilinear object drawn at equal angles; dimensions along them are same scale

continued overleaf

continued

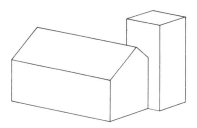

dimetric projection: dimensions to same scale on two of axes, different on third

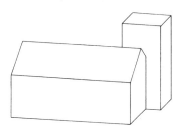

trimetric projection: dimensions to different scale along each axis

AZERTY keyboard	acronym denoting standard keyboard layout, derived from order of characters on first alphabetic line for many European countries, as compared to 'QWERTY keyboard' → used in US and UK
azure	term used for lighter tints of blue 'laid' and 'wove' papers →

B

B (= bulb)	in photography, shutter setting on camera that holds shutter open as long as exposure release is held down
back (of book)	that edge of any book at which leaves are secured (see 'book'), also called 'spine' or 'shelfback'; may also refer (confusingly) to pages toward end of book, especially periodical
back clipping plane	same as 'yon plane' →
back end plane (computers)	one that is designed to function at end of computer-controlled process, eg: 'graph plotter' →
back margin	see 'page'
back matter (of book)	US term for 'end-matter' →
back number	any issue of periodical prior to current one

back projection	projecting transparencies onto back of translucent screen, fine cloth or frosted glass; used for faking backgrounds in studio photography:

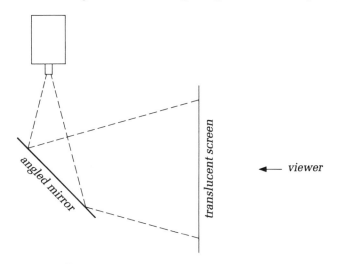

back-step collation	see 'collation'
back-up, backing-up	printing second, or reverse, side of sheet; also known as 'perfecting'
backbone (of book)	same as 'spine' →
background (computers)	function permitting one task to take place while operator is performing another
backing store (computers)	data store of larger capacity and slower 'access time' → than 'memory/main memory' →
backslanted	said of typeface that inclines to left:

ABCdefghijklmn

backward reader	name given by periodical publishers to those frustrating and numerous readers who will insist on flipping through pages from back to front
bad break	unsuitable 'end-of-line decision' → usually resulting from inadequate 'h & j code' →
band aid (computers)	synonym for 'patch' →; term more common in US
bang	slang for exclamation mark
bank paper	uncoated paper produced for typewriting, similar to bond but lighter; used for carbon copies

19

banker envelope	commonest pattern, having opening and flap on longer edge, thus:

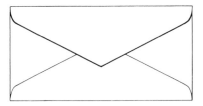

banner	newspaper headline running across whole width of page
bar code	pre-printed pattern of vertical lines that is 'read' by computer-linked optical sensor; such devices are now increasingly in use at checkout points of supermarkets for stock control and ordering, and pattern is devised to conform either with Universal Product Code (UPC) or European Article Number (EANC), which identify product category, manufacturer and product ID number:

bar graph/chart	'coordinate graph' → in which values are represented by vertical or horizontal bars, as distinct from line graph; also known as 'columnar graph': if more than one value is to be included, 'segmented bar graph' may be used:

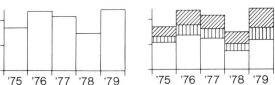

barn doors	in photography, apparatus fixed to spotlight or floodlamp to control direction of light:

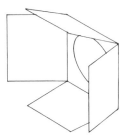

barred d another name for obsolete character 'eth' →

barrel distortion typical distortion of CRT image:
(computer graphics)

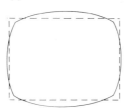

barrel printer see 'computer output devices'
(computer graphics)

baryta paper special matt-coated paper suitable for 'repro proofs' →

base synonym for 'radix' →

base alignment typical function in 'photocomposition' → system whereby different type sizes are automatically aligned on 'base line' →:

economic on-line information for the chemical industry.

base artwork artwork to which further components (such as screened halftone positives) are to be added before reproduction

base film in photomechanical reproduction, material to which film positives are stripped in order to make contact film for platemaking

baseline horizontal line connecting the bottoms of those lower-case characters which do not have descenders, from which is derived 'baseline-to-baseline' method of measuring line intervals; see also 'x-height'

BASIC see 'computer languages'

basic size US term for sheet size used to calculate 'basis weight' →

basis weight US term for weight of 'ream' → of paper to given standard size of sheet; usual standard for book and periodical paper is 25 × 38in, for cover stock 20 × 26in, and for stationery paper 17 × 22in

bastard size any matter used in printing that is of non-standard size

bastard title same as 'half-title' →

batch processing grouping data for input as single chunk when convenient for
(computers) processing, as against 'real-time processing' →

batter (as noun) in letterpress, damaged type or block

baud rate measure of speed at which data is transmitted in telecommunications

Bauhaus	literally, German for 'Building House': most famous design school of inter-war years, started in 1919 at Weimar, Germany, under Walter Gropius; moved to Dessau in 1925, Berlin in 1932, finally closed by Nazis in 1933
BCD	initials of *binary code decimal* (see 'binary notation')
beard (of type)	in UK, space extending from base line of typeface to lower limit of body as it appears on page; in US, synonym for 'bevel' (see 'type')
bed (of press)	flat surface on which matter to be printed is laid
begin even	instruction to printer: start copy full out, without indent; not used in US, where 'begin flush left' is preferred
bell character (computers)	one in a terminal keyboard array used to sound bell alerting operator to some condition in routine
bells and whistles (computers)	attention-getting noises emanating from computers, signalling some significant stage or event
below-the-line	advertising term used to describe those items in an advertising budget that are not strictly advertisements, eg: brochures
belt/bed plotter (computers)	development of 'drum plotter' →, fitted with continuous belt in place of drum and with vertical plotting surface
belt press	variant of 'rotary press' →, designed primarily for bookwork in which flexible letterpress plates are mounted on two belts that print both sides of web of paper and feed it, cut into four page sections, directly into binder
benchmark (computers)	calculation of effectiveness of computer system by running typical task through it
Berne Convention	original copyright agreement of 1886, revised most recently in Paris, 1971, to which UK adheres but not US (see 'Universal Copyright Convention 1952')
Beta	video cassette recording system (originally known as Betamax) competing with VHS system →
bevel (of type)	sloping surface that extends from shoulder to face (see 'type')
bevel (of letterpress plate)	another name for 'flange' →
bf	instruction to printer on manuscript, typescript or proof: set in 'bold face' (more common in newspaper publishing in UK, but universal in US)
BFMP	see 'British Printing Industries Federation'

bible paper	synonym for 'india paper' →
biblio, biblio page	common name for page in book 'prelims' → that contains publishing history of book and publisher's imprint; but beware of confusion with 'bibliography' →
bibliography	list of authors, titles and publishers of books and periodicals relevant to particular subject; may form self-contained publication in its own right but is more normally part of 'end-matter' → of another book
bidirectional printing (computers)	alternation of printing consecutive lines in computer print-out device, thus avoiding need for return to beginning of line
Bildschirmtext	name of public 'videotex' → system in Federal Republic of Germany
bimetal plate	long-lasting printing plate in which printing area is of copper and non-printing area of steel or aluminium; used for runs of 500,000 and over
binary code	system that can convert anything expressible as numbers or as symbolic logic into a sequence of 'yes/no' questions and answers for storage in, and retrieval from, a computer
binary digit	in computer usage, basic unit (either 1 or 0) of 'binary code' system →; usually abbreviated as 'bit'
binary notation	two-state arithmetic employed in electronic computers because of 'on-off' modes typical of certain kinds of electronic circuit; digits used are 1 (on) and 0 (off) and values are represented by position of digits, thus:

```
0   0   0   0   position
8   4   2   1   value
```

decimal values may then be expressed in this way:

decimal	binary	decimal	binary	decimal	binary
0	0000	6	0110	12	1100
1	0001	7	0111	13	1101
2	0010	8	1000	14	1110
3	0011	9	1001	15	1111
4	0100	10	1010		
5	0101	11	1011		

binary coded decimal (BCD) system employs groups of four 'bits' each:

	thousands	hundreds	tens	units
8219 =	1000	0010	0001	1001
4601 =	0100	0110	0000	0001

binder's brass/die	metal plate incorporating raised design for stamping binding of 'cased book' → (also called 'stamping brass')
binding edge	that edge of book at which sheets are secured; same as 'spine' and 'back edge'

binding methods   most common binding methods are:

loose-leaf methods

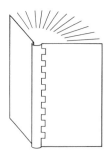

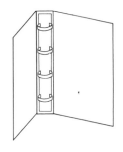

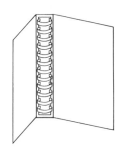

plastic grip spine   *plastic comb spine*   *post or ring binder*   *multiple ring binder*

permanent binding methods

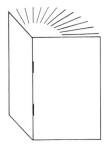

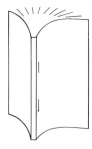

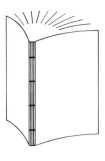

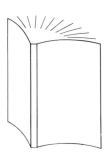

saddle-stitched   *side-stitched*   *section-sewn*   *perfect (unsewn)*

bit (computers)   useful contraction of *binary digit'* →

bit density   measure, usually in bits per inch (bpi) of density of data on magnetic
(computers)   disks or magnetic tape (typically around 1,600 bpi)

bit depth (computers)   measure of number of bits representing colours and their intensity, in
'frame buffer' →; typically, frame buffer 8 bits deep will store 256
colours

bit map (computers)   record of specific image made in digitized form for storage in, and
retrieval from, computer

bit pad (computers)   same as 'digitizing pad' → and 'tablet'

BL   initials of *British Library*

black crush   in TV, electronic effect that converts live action image into total
black/white contrast, without half tones

black face   same as 'bold face' →

black letter	style of typeface once widely used in northern Europe, closely based on broad-nib pen style; also known as 'gothic' → in UK, 'Old English' and 'text type' in US:

𝔄𝔅𝔆𝔇𝔈𝔉𝔊𝔥𝔍𝔎
black and turquoise

BLAISE, Blaise	acronym for *B*ritish *L*ibrary *A*utomated *I*nformation *Se*rvice
blanket cylinder	in 'offset' →, one that takes ink image from 'plate cylinder' and transfers it to paper or other printing material by means of thick sheet of rubberized fabric
blanket-to-blanket	typical feature of 'web-fed offset' → press whereby both sides of paper are printed simultaneously from two 'blanket cylinders' →
bleach-out	same as 'line conversion' →; also, under-developed photoprint with 'ghost' image, used as basis for line drawing
bleed	to run line or halftone image off edge of trimmed page or sheet; it is usual to allow 3mm (in US ⅛in) for this:

blind-embossed	relief impression made with die-stamp that is not inked or foiled
blind folio	page of book that does not have page number (folio) but which is included in pagination, eg: title page
blind keyboard	one in which no visual copy is produced at time of inputting; quicker to operate but more liable to error
blind P	reversed P with filled-in counter, used as 'paragraph mark' →
Blissymbols	set of 100 signs devised by Charles Bliss, first published 1949 as basis of international non-phonetic language system but not given practical application until 1971

blister pack	transparent plastic bubble fixed to flat backing card, enclosing product; may be shaped to fit closely
block	line or halftone plate mounted to 'type-height' → for use in letterpress printing (term not common in US)
block (computers)	group of units of information handled as one, particularly in 'magnetic disk' →
block book	one printed from page-sized wood blocks from which letters were carved in relief; fore-runner of movable-type book
block diagram	1) one devised to represent functional relationships:

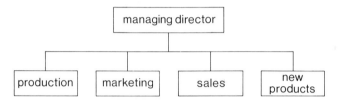

2) one using square blocks as units to represent comparisons of quantities:

3) one used by cartographers to show geological and/or surface relief of particular portion of land:

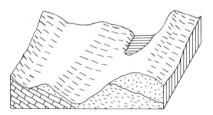

blocking	stamping image onto case of book or pack by means of blocking, or binder's brass; may be inked, foiled or left blind (ie: without either); known in US as 'stamping' or 'tooling'
blocking (computer graphics)	synonym for 'batch processing' →

blockmaker	one who makes letterpress plates by 'photoengraving' → known in US as 'photoengraver'
blow back	enlargement on paper of image stored on 'microform' →
blow-moulding	forcing air between two sheets of plastic to form hollow shape; thus:

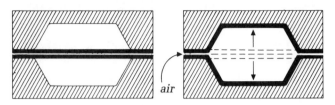

blow-up	photographic enlargement, usually from smaller print via copy negative
blue-skying	engaging in fanciful, optimistic speculation about future possibilities
blues, blueprints	proofs, having white lines against blue ground, intended for preliminary checking purposes; largely superseded by 'diazo' prints →
blurb	brief summary of contents of a book and/or biography of author printed on jacket or soft cover
board	paper-based material of weight greater than 200g/m² (UK) or 10 points (US)
body	main part of piece of 'type' →
body copy/matter/type	text matter used in main body of work, as distinct from headings or other display matter
body paper	base for 'coated paper' →
body size	measurement in points of body of type as cast; may be slightly larger than 'type size' →
bold, bold face	heavier version of normal weight of typeface:

Optima **Optima Bold**

bolt	any folded edge of printed section (signature) which is to be trimmed (ie: not back fold)
bond paper	grade of paper made for writing and typewriting, but which can also be used for printing; lighter weights are called 'bank'

book	any leaved work that is bound; parts of typical book are:

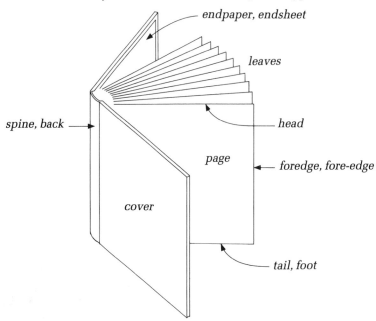

book jacket	printed paper outer, wrapped around cased cover of hard-backed book; also known as 'dust jacket' or 'wrapper'
book proof	'sheet proofs' → made up in book form for final approval
book sizes	see 'paper sizes and subdivisions'
Boolean algebra (computers)	one using operators such as AND, OR, NOT, IF, THEN and EXCEPT to express logical relationships; widely used in computer programs (named after its progenitor, UK mathematician George Boole)
boot (computers)	slang for starting up computer
bootstrap (computers)	program for starting up computer
border (type)	ornamental type matter consisting of single pieces, cast to standard body sizes, arranged in strip form:

Boring's mother-in-law	famous ambiguous image devised by US psychologist E G Boring, which sometimes looks like old women, sometimes like young girl:

Boris	Canadian 'videotex' → system
bottom out	US term for adjustment of typeset matter to eliminate 'widow' →
bounce-lighting	in studio photography, lighting subject solely or mainly by indirect lighting reflected from walls, ceilings or specially made reflectors
boundary fill (VDU)	filling 'region' → with tone or colour by identifying 'picture elements' → within boundary
bowl (of type)	curving stroke of type character enclosing counter (see 'type')
box	type or other graphic matter enclosed by rule border to separate it from other matter; also, that border itself
box enamel	'enamel paper' → specially made for box covers
boxed mode	form of 'videotex' → display in which characters of one tone/colour are shown on a rectangle of another and superimposed on an analog transmission; used for visual translation of foreign-language interview, etc
boxing (computers)	using boxes to select specific components of computer graphics displayed on screen
bpi (computers)	initials of 'bits per inch': measurement of density with which data can be recorded on magnetic tape (see 'bit')
BPOP	initials of bulk packed on palettes
brace	typographic sign used to link several items, thus:

$$\left.\begin{array}{l}\text{FARMDOC}\\\text{AGDOC}\\\text{PLASDOC}\end{array}\right\}\text{included in Central Patents Index from 1970}$$

bracketed (type)	used to describe those serifs which are joined to main part (stem) of type character by continuous curve or bracket:

brackets	pair of signs like this (parentheses or curved brackets) or this [square brackets]; used to separate matter they enclose from context
BRAD	initials of '*B*ritish *R*ate *a*nd *D*ata', regular publication giving those details of national and provincial newspapers published in UK which are relevant to placing of advertisements
branch (computers)	point in program at which choice must be made to take one of two or more possible routes
brass	engraved plate used by bookbinder for 'blocking' →; known in US as 'binder's die'
brayer	small hand roller used for inking when making proofs
break up for colour	instruction to printer: break up forme which is to be printed in more than one colour, making separate formes for each colour
breve	curved line over vowel indicating that it is 'short', thus: nĭppy
Brightype	trade name for technique of deriving photographic image from letterpress type or plates, by spraying on black lacquer, then removing it from face only, so providing reflective surface for photography
Bristol board	fine pasteboard with smooth surface, ideal for drawing up artwork
British Imperial System	traditional system of units of measurement, using inches and feet, pints and gallons, ounces and pounds; 'US Customary System' → is very similar but not identical
British Printing Industries Federation	employers' organization and trade association for general printing industry in UK, founded in 1900 as British Federation of Master Printers (BFMP) and renamed in 1974
broadsheet newspaper	traditional, large format paper, as compared with 'tabloid'
broadside, broadsheet	any sheet in its basic, uncut size; one that is printed on one side only

broke	sub-standard paper separated from good stock after manufacture; usually marked xxx
bromide	short for 'bromide print': normal kind of photographic print; often used for pre-platemaking proofs in photolitho, hence 'bromide proofs'
bronzing	obtaining metallic effect in printing by first applying an adhesive layer, then dusting it with metallic powder
brownprint	same as 'Van Dyke print' →
brush (computer graphics)	interactive function that imparts line of varying thickness to graphic display on screen
BS	prefix used to denote standard set by British Standards Institution; there are shoals of these things in printing and publishing – far too many to list here
BTX	abbreviation for '*B*ildschirm*text* →
bubble memory (computers)	see 'magnetic bubble memory'
buckle folding	method whereby printing sheet is buckled on metal plate, as compared with 'knife folding' →
buckram	sized bookbinders' cloth
buffer (computers)	temporary storage device in which data can be accumulated before further processing
buffered keyboard	one devised to prevent jamming due to inexpert typing, by delaying print-action
bulk	relationship between weight and thickness of sheet of paper; less dense the material, greater the bulk
bulk after printing (of paper)	reference to change in 'bulk' → of paper after being flattened when passing through press
bulking dummy	book made up with blank sheets to show 'bulk' →
bulking index	US term denoting product of sheet thickness in inches by 'basis weight' →
bulking number	US term denoting number of sheets per inch of thickness (assuming standard pressure)
bulldog	slang term for first edition of daily newspaper
bullet	type ornament in form of large dot, used to itemize or emphasize

bullseye	synonym for 'hickie' →
bundle	US term for two 'reams' → of paper, that is, 1,000 sheets
Bureau of Standards	US government agency responsible for standards of measurement and performance
burning out	cleaning up portions of litho plate by use of opaque mask
burst binding	nicking back edges of 'gathered sections/signatures' → so as to be able to impregnate them with adhesive more effectively
bus (computers)	structured route whereby signals move between separate components of computer system
butt splicing	in film and tape editing, making joins without overlaps by means of adhesive tape or heat fusion
buyout	US term for printing operation (eg: typesetting) that is not executed in printer's own works
by-line	typeline giving name of author(s) of periodical or newspaper article
byte (computers)	in computer jargon, group of 'bits' → – usually 6 or 8 – that make up one alphabetic, numerical or special character

C

©	copyright mark, used to conform with 'Universal Copyright Convention 1952' →
cable release	in photography, flexible extension exposure release for operating shutter with less risk of camera shake during exposure
CAD, cad	acronym for *c*omputer *a*ided *d*esign
CADAM, cadam	acronym for *c*omputer *a*ided *d*esign *a*nd *m*anufacture
CADCAM, CAD/ CAM, cadcam	acronym for *c*omputer *a*ided *d*esign/*c*omputer *a*ided *m*anufacture
CADD	initials of *c*omputer *a*ided *d*esign and *d*raughting
CAE	initials of *c*omputer *a*ided *e*ngineering
calenders	metal rollers through which paper is passed in order to give it smoothly polished (calendered) surface during making process
california case	type case designed to include both 'upper case' → and 'lower case' →

caliper	thickness of sheet, especially of board, measured in microns (millionths of a metre) or mils (thousands of an inch)
calligraphic display (computer graphics)	occasional synonym for 'vector display' →
calligraphy	fine handwriting
CAM, cam	acronym for *c*omputer *a*ided *m*anufacture
cameo (type)	applied to those typefaces in which characters are reversed white out of solid or shaded ground:

SPECIAL NEWS

camera-ready artwork	any 'camera-ready copy' → that includes hand work; also known, especially in US, as 'mechanical'
camera-ready copy	any matter prepared for reproduction that is ready to go before 'process camera' →
camera-ready paste-up	any camera-ready artwork that involves pasting together of number of component parts
camera shake	greatest enemy of sharp, crisp negative making: all shots not requiring hand holding should be made from tripod mounting to eliminate camera shake, especially at slower shutter speeds
camera types	main camera types are:

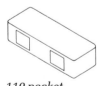

110 pocket

110 pocket rangefinder

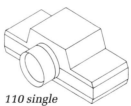

110 single lens reflex

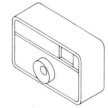

126 simple

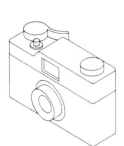

35mm compact

35mm compact rangefinder

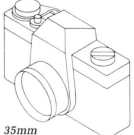

35mm single lens reflex

continued overleaf

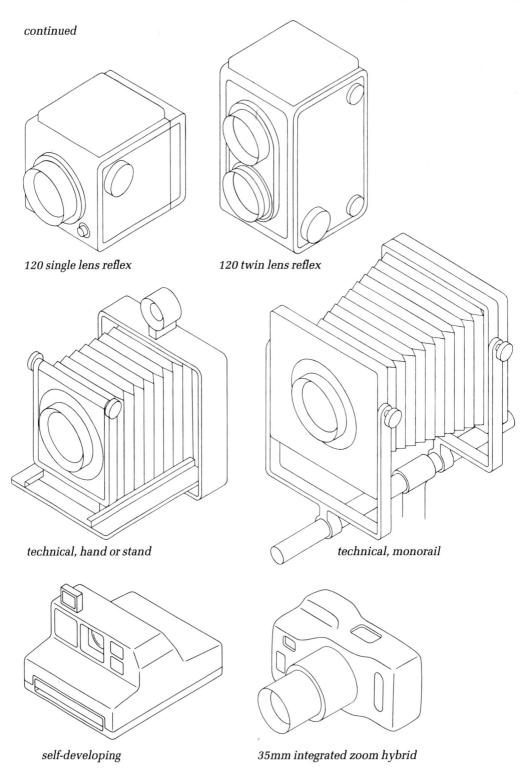

120 single lens reflex

120 twin lens reflex

technical, hand or stand

technical, monorail

self-developing

35mm integrated zoom hybrid

CAMIS	acronym for *c*omputer-*a*ssisted *m*ake-up *i*maging *s*ystem
cancel (as noun)	reprinted leaf or section to be substituted for existing part of book which was printed in error
cancelled numeral (figure)	type character consisting of numeral with diagonal stroke through it; used in mathematical texts
canned paragraph	in word-processing, pre-setting portion of text which recurs frequently, for more rapid handling
cap line	imaginary horizontal line connecting tops of line of caps, often (but not necessarily) corresponding to 'ascender line' →:

abcde ABCD

ascender line
cap line

capital, cap	upper-case letters, as A, B, C, D; also known as 'majuscule'
Captains	acronym for *C*haracter *a*nd *P*attern *T*elephone *A*ccess *I*nformation *N*etwork *S*ystem (phew!): Japanese 'videotex' → system
caption	descriptive phrase, sentence or paragraph placed below, beside or above illustration; also known in US as 'cutline'
captured keystrokes	input to machine such as 'word processor' → that have been appropriated, usually in magnetic disk form, for use in another machine, such as photocomposer
carbon arc lamp	light source used in photomechanical reproduction and cineprojection, now largely replaced by 'metal halide lamp' →
carbonless copy paper	same as 'ncr' paper →
carbro process	one devised for correction of colour values in 'photomechanical process' → before positive stage
cardinal numbers	one, two, three and so on, as distinct from ordinal numbers, first, second, third
caret, caret mark	sign used in proof correction to show that something is to be inserted:

carful   e∧

carry forward	same as 'take over' →
cartesian coordinates	see 'coordinate graph'
cartesian graph	same as 'coordinate graph' →
cartogram	map that incorporates statistical information

carton	container designed to lie flat until required for use, as distinct from rigid box
cartridge (paper)	closely woven, well-sized paper produced in heavy substances for drawing and offset litho printing; best grades are made on 'twin-wire' machines →
case	stiff cover of book; also, container for type
case fraction	one cast as whole type, as distinct from 'piece fraction' → or 'full-sized fraction' →; also known as 'solid fraction'
cased/case-bound book	one with stiff cover as distinct from one with soft cover; same as 'hard back' or 'hard cover' book
cast coated	coated paper or board with exceptionally thick, glossy coating, achieved by adding second coating to pre-coated base and passing it round highly polished, heated drum to get high finish
casting-off	estimating amount of space manuscript will occupy when typeset in certain typeface and measure:

The total number of characters in a manuscript is calculated by counting the number of characters and spaces in an average line length and multiplying this figure by the total number of lines in the manuscript. It is then possible to determine the number of lines of typesetting by dividing the number of characters in the manuscript by the average number per line in a given typeface and measure.

$$\begin{array}{r} 55 \\ \times 7 \\ \hline 385 \end{array}$$

A more accurate cast-off may be obtained by counting the characters in each paragraph separately, so that the short lines at the ends of the paragraphs are taken individually into account.

$$\begin{array}{r} 55 \\ \times 3 \\ \hline 165 \\ +12 \\ \hline 177 \end{array}$$

Absolute accuracy, as against an approximation, is achieved by subtracting the number of characters by which a line of manuscript falls short of the norm and adding on any by which a line may extend beyond the norm.

$$\begin{array}{r} 55 \\ \times 3 \\ \hline 165 \\ -2 \\ \hline 163 \\ +3 \\ \hline 166 \\ +39 \\ \hline 205 \end{array}$$

CAT	initials of *c*omputer-*a*ided *t*ypesetting
catch-up	unintended image transferred from litho plate resulting from improper application of ink and water
catchline	identifying number and title set at top of each 'galley proof' →
cathode ray tube	see 'CRT'
CATV	initials of *c*ommunity *a*ntenna *tele*vision (cable television)
CBMS	initials of *c*omputer-*b*ased *m*essage *s*ystem

CCD initials of *c*harge *c*oupled *d*evice, key component in digital imaging system of 'scanner' →

CCITT initials of *C*omité *C*onsultatif *I*nternational *T*éléphonique et *T*élé-graphique: UN authority on telecommunications

CCR initials of *c*omplementary *c*olour *r*emoval; same as 'achromatic colour correction' →

CCTV initials of *c*losed *c*ircuit *tele*vision →

CD/ROM (computers) acronym for *c*ompact *d*isk/*r*ead-*o*nly *m*emory (see 'ROM'); one using optical laser techniques

CdS meter see 'exposure meter'

cedilla c see 'accented (diacritical) signs'

Ceefax (= see facts) name of British Broadcasting Corporation's system for transmitting 'teletext' → news and information

cel in film animation, transparent surface of same proportion as frame of cinefilm, on which one stage of animation sequence is drawn; of standard size and punched to fit over register pins:

cel sandwich in film animation, superimposition of up to four cels for simultaneous photography

cell in 'photogravure' →, tiny recessed dot carrying inked image, similar to halftone dot

cellophane proprietary name for brand of cellulose film; transparent, grease-proof material used mainly for wrapping

cellulose fibrous material, originally derived from linen or cotton but now from woodpulp, used as basis for papermaking

centered dot	US expression for raised point used for decimal notation
central processor unit (computers)	see 'CPU'
centre fold/spread	central opening of section across two pages
centre notes	those inserted between columns of type on page
centre of projection	synonym for 'station point' →, commonly used in 3D systems in computer graphics
cf	abbreviation for *confer,* Latin for 'compare'; used in footnotes
chad	paper waste produced when holes are punched in paper tape or cards
chain lines/marks	widely spaced watermark lines in 'laid' paper → running at right angles to closely spaced 'laid' lines
chain printer	see 'computer output devices'
chalking	printing defect which results in loose ink on surface of paper
chancery italic	roman handwriting style of 15–16th century, on which cursive (italic) typefaces were based:

Dele uarie forti de littere poi‚che in queſto Tratta‐
tello trouerai‚ſe io ti uoleſſi ad una per una defcriuere

chapel	old term for association of journeyman printers, now applied to local branches of printers' and journalists' trades unions
chapter drop	position on page of book at which text begins below chapter head, as distinct from standard run of text:

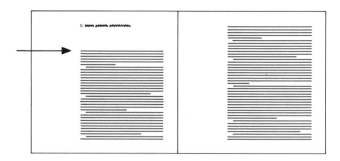

character	any individual letter, figure, punctuation mark or sign in typeface

character assembly	blanket term covering all methods by which letters, figures, special characters and spaces are generated for reproduction; more suitable than 'typesetting' for such techniques as photocomposition
character bit-map (computers)	'bit-map' → delineating shape of display or print character in digitized form
character count	sum of characters in line or paragraph or piece of copy
character generator	central part of computer-aided CRT photocomposition system; two basic types are (a) character projection and (b) character formation
character pair kerning	same as 'kerning pairs' →
character printer	output device that prints characters consecutively in line from left to right, as in conventional typewriter or teleprinter, as against 'line-printer' →
character reader (computers)	input device that converts human-readable characters into machine-readable language, as in 'OCR' → and 'MICR' →
character set	set of letters, numerals (figures), punctuation marks, reference marks and other signs, chosen or designed for particular system or keyboard; in typesetting, character set is known as 'fount' (UK) or 'font' (US)
character space (computers)	that occupied by character in 'videotex' → system
chase	in letterpress, metal frame used to hold and secure matter for printing; hence 'in chase' (ready to print)
check digit	one used in 'bar code' → permitting computer sensor to check for correct interpretation of coded data; last number in 'ISBN' → is also check digit
chemical pulp	wood pulp chemically treated, as distinct from mechanical pulp; used for better quality printing papers
chemical transfer process	same as 'DTR' →
cheque/check paper	one with surface that will betray attempts to alter writing
chip (electronics)	colloquial name for 'silicon-chip' →; also known as 'micro-chip'
chord (geometry)	straight line joining two points of arc:

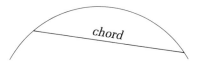

chord keyboard
(computers)

input device with five keys similar in shape to piano keys, that may be operated singly or in combination:

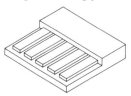

choropleth map

one that represents different density values of specific areas calculated on basis of average numbers per unit of area:

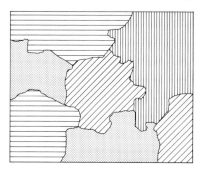

chroma

degree of intensity or purity of any colour; also, in TV, abbreviation for 'chrominance': colour component of video signal

Chroma Key

trade name now commonly applied to television presentation technique of 'colour separation overlay' →

chrome

US slang for 'colour transparency' →

chromo

one-sided art paper used mainly for proofing

chromolithography

traditional technique of drawing images on stone ('autolithography') in matched sets to produce multi-coloured picture; hand-drawn colour lithography persisted to mid-20th century, especially for posters

Cibachrome-A

speedy colour print system working directly positive-to-positive

cicero

'Didot' → equivalent of 'pica' → as unit of measurement: 4.500mm (see also *'corps douze'*)

CIF

initials of *c*arriage, *f*reight, *i*nsurance

CIM

initials of *c*omputer *i*nput *m*icrofilm

CIP

initials of *C*ataloguing *I*n *P*ublication, program run by US Library of Congress jointly with British Library to establish classified data on new books prior to publication; this is then inserted on imprint/ copyright page of book in question

circuit diagram   representation of components and their connexions composed as specific functional design, usually electric or electronic

circular graph   one in which values are plotted from central point along radiating axes, forming closed curves:

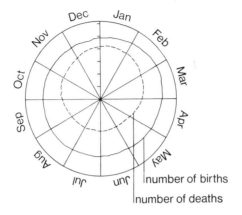

circumflex   see 'accented (diacritical) signs'

clapper-board   in cinefilm, hand-operated device giving information about title, slate number and take number, which is filmed briefly at start of each take; hinged upper portion is clapped down to aid sound/picture synchronization

clarendon   family of typefaces having characteristics both of roman and slab-serif:

ABDegh

clean proof   one containing no errors or corrections

clicker   slang for compositor who has responsibility of passing out copy for setting by fellow comps

client   person who wants everything yesterday and at half-price

client's rough   common misnomer for 'presentation visual' →

clipping
(computer graphics)   truncating 'primitives' → which would otherwise extend beyond boundary of 'window' →

close up   instruction to typesetter to reduce or eliminate space between characters, words or lines of text

**closed circuit
television**   system in which signal is fed to limited number of viewing monitors by cable

closed 'h'	lower-case italic 'h' in which short stroke curves inwards, thus:

h

closed section/ signature	one in which folds or bolts are left uncut
club line	short (because indented) line at beginning of paragraph when appearing at foot of column
clump	in letterpress, spacing material of 6pt body or thicker (also called 'slug' in US); sometimes known as 'reglet', especially when made of wood
clutch pencil	mechanical pencil so called because of method by which lead is gripped and released
CMC7	character set designed for 'MICR' →
CMY colour system	one based on subtractive primaries cyan/magenta/yellow, as contrasted to 'RGB colour system' →, see also 'subtractive colour mixing'
coarse screen	any halftone screen up to 85 lines to inch (34 lines to centimetre)
coated paper	one having covering of coating slip made from china clay to provide fine finish suitable for 'halftone' → reproduction; may be 'machine-' →, 'blade-' → or 'cast-coated' →
COBOL	see 'computer languages'
cock-and-hens	brace composed of several pieces of type joined together, central piece is cock, end pieces are hens
cock-up numeral (figure) or letter	same as 'superior numeral (figure) or letter' →
cocked-up initial	one projecting above line of type on which it stands, thus:

Punched card data processing is based upon the unit record
one card is utilized for encoding the essential data of each tra
data are recorded and verified through some type of data rec
automatic punching, as indicated in the previous chapter. The

code conversion	operation sometimes required when using 'word-processor' → material for typesetting
code key	same as 'function key' →

codec	acronym of *code-de*coder, device for converting analog signals to digital signals and vice versa
col	abbreviation for 'column'
cold composition	imprecise and regrettable term intended to cover any composition produced by typewriters but extended to include photocomposition
cold melt	adhesive such as polyvinyl alcohol (PVA) which does not need heat; used in book binding
cold type	another loose term meaning same as 'cold composition'
collation	to check correct order of printed sections (signatures) after gathering; also used (incorrectly) to include whole process of gathering and collation, especially of single sheets; collating marks are often printed in stepped sequence on back folds of sections (known as 'back-steps') so that any misplacement is easily spotted:

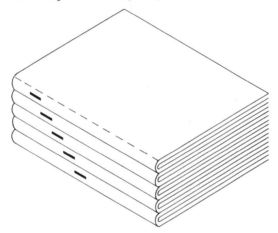

collotype	photomechanical, planographic printing process using gelatin covered plate without halftone dot; very fine reproduction but only suited to short runs
colophon	1) inscription formerly placed at end of book by publisher, title, printer, publisher, date and place of publication, and emblem; now more often shown on verso of title page 2) latterly, applied to emblem itself
Coloroid colour system	one devised by A Nemcsics in 1980 as alternative to 'Munsell colour system' →
colour (of typeface)	degree of lightness or heaviness in appearance of particular typeface
colour bars	in four-colour processing, proofs should contain standard sets of bars devised to show strength of ink across plate, register, etc

colour cast	undue dominance of one colour in colour photograph or reproduction
colour-coding	distinguishing between groups of products, printed forms, signs or what-have-you by giving them different colours; popular technique of doubtful effectiveness (what about differing light conditions and people with varying degrees of colour blindness?)
colour correction	adjustment of colour values for faithful reproduction, either during initial stage of processing, or subsequently as result of proof reading
colour filter	sheet of gelatin, glass or plastic used in making 'colour separation' →
colour look-up table (computer graphics)	part of memory in 'frame buffer' → containing values of colour content
colour negative film	film in which colours are in negative form after processing
colour positives	set of screened four-colour separations with positive image, used for deep-etch litho platemaking
colour reversal film	film in which colours are in positive (natural) form after processing
colour rotation	printing sequence for inks in 'four colour process' →
colour scanning	using electronic device to scan original subject (whether opaque or transparent) and derive 'colour separations' → for manufacture of four colour process plates
colour separation	photographic filtering process whereby colours of an original are separated out for reproduction
colour separation overlay	original name for television technique in which one camera is directed at presenter located in front of blue background while another camera is pointed at film or video displaying live action sequence that is imposed on blue ground; now known under trade name of Chroma Key
colour separations	see 'separation artwork'
colour stat	rough colour print suitable for use in presentation
colour swatch	patch of colour (usually, but not necessarily, part of colour matching system) that is used as guide for reproduction
colour temperature	expression in degrees Kelvin (°K) of colour quality of light source, derived from appearance of light radiated by black body heated to incandescence
colour transparency	colour photograph (usually positive) on transparent film
column balancing	highly suspect feature in 'page make-up terminal' → whereby columns of type that would otherwise be uneven in length are fiddled to achieve evenness

columnar graph	see 'bar graph/chart'
COM	acronym for *c*omputer *o*utput on *m*icrofilm
combination plate	see 'line-and-halftone plate'
coming and going	printing 'imposition' → method whereby pages are printed head to head so that one set of plates can make two impressions on same side of sheet
command	operating instructions to computer
commercial A	type character meaning 'at': @
communicating word processor	one that is connected by means of established network so as to permit rapid inter-office or inter-company text transmission; abbreviated as 'CWP'
communication theory	mathematical theory relating to least number of decisions required to identify one message from given set of messages
comp	common abbreviation for 'comprehensive': US term for 'presentation visual' →
comp list	slang term for list of persons or companies who are to receive complimentary copies of any periodical
COMPAC	acronym for *c*omputer *o*utput *m*icrofilm *pac*kage
compact-source iodide	see 'metal halide lamp'
compose	to put together type and rules by hand or machine
composing room	that part of printing works where type is set and made up
composing stick	implement for setting type in by hand
composite print	in cinefilm, same as 'married print' →
composition size	any size of type up to 14pt used primarily for text setting
compositor, comp	one who composes and imposes type; also called 'typographer' in US
compound table	in film animation, US term for 'rostrum' table →
computer	electronic machine designed to receive and process 'data' → so as to have information available on demand or as means of controlling some other machine; main types are 'analog' → and 'digital' →
computer console	unit used for all manual communication with computer; contains display of information and has keyboard for input of instructions

computer graphics	graphic presentations made by means of computer, whether on screen or 'graph plotter' →, originally applied to line-drawing technique using 'vector display' →, now includes image generation by 'raster display' → and is being extended to 'liquid-crystal display' → and 'plasma panel display' →
computer graphics camera	one specially designed to make photographic records from electronically displayed pictures
computer input devices	those by which human instructions or queries are made intelligible to computer, available in following types: punched card, paper tape, teletypewriter, optical character recognition (OCR) encoder, magnetic ink character recognition (MICR) encoder, visual display unit (VDU) with light-pen, digitizing pad (tablet) or table
computer output devices	those by which information from computer is made intelligible to humans, available in following types: teletypewriter, high-speed impact line-printers (barrel or chain), non-impact printers (ink-jet, electrothermal, electrostatic, dot-matrix or xerographic), graph plotters (flatbed or drum), visual display unit (VDU), microfilm
computer languages	several languages have been developed specially for use in computer programming, among which are ALGOL (*Algo*rithmic *Language*); COBOL (*Common Business Oriented Language*); FORTRAN (*Formula Translator*); PL/1 (*Programming Language/One*); BASIC (*Beginners' All-purpose Symbolic Instruction Code*); Pascal
computer micrographics	system for handling 'COM' → or 'CIM' →
computerized composition	character assembly with aid of computer which is programmed to process some, or all, functions after keyboarding and up to setting
concertina fold	method of folding paper in which each fold is in opposite direction to previous one (see 'folding methods'); same as 'accordion fold'
condensed	used to describe narrower version of normal typeface:

ABCDEFGHabcdefghi

cone of vision (perspective)	in 'perspective projections' →, configuration formed by convergence of 'visual rays' onto 'station point'
C1S	initials of *c*oated one (*1*) *s*ide, as in 'coated paper' → or board used for cover
configuration (general)	form of arrangement or design of related parts, where outlined may be significant, as in dress pattern, or not, as in electrical circuit
configuration (computers)	form of arrangement of units which comprise computer system

conic sections   curves derived from planes intersecting a cone; they are:

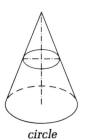

circle

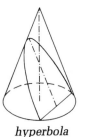

ellipse

hyperbola

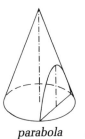

parabola

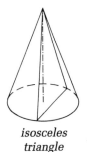

isosceles triangle

conical projections   group of projections of Earth in which plane of projection is cone
(global)   which touches globe along parallel:

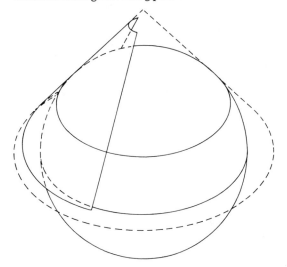

console (computers)   general name for unit used for manual communication with computer

constat   abbreviation for 'continuous stationery' →

contact print   photographic print made direct from film positive or negative without enlargement

contact printing frame   same as 'vacuum frame' →

contact screen   another name for 'halftone screen' (see 'halftone process')

continuous fold   system of folding paper from roll in series of concertina folds (see 'folding methods')

continuous stationery   continuous paper supply folded into pack by means of perforations, provided with sprocket holes for automatic feeding through print unit

continuous-tone copy	any original in which the gradation of tones requires photomechanical halftone processing
contre-jour	in photography, shooting with light source in front of camera lens rather than to one side or to rear:

control characters (computers)	one in 'character set' → whose relevant key on input keyboard does not represent printed or displayed alphanumeric character but which initiates activity such as 'scrolling' →; also known as 'functional character'
control loop	in 'ergonomics' →, symbolic relationship between operator and machine he/she controls:

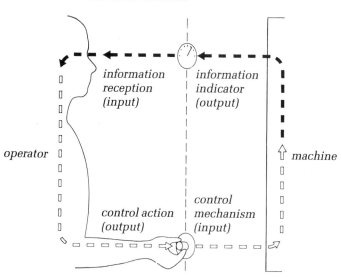

control tape (computers)	in computer-driven 'photocomposition' →, one establishing parameters such as measure and format; superseded by disk

converging verticals   familiar visual phenomenon in which parallel vertical lines appear to converge (as when tall building is viewed from below); corrected by use of 'rising front' → on camera:

convertible press   one that can print two colours on one side of sheet or one colour on two sides

converting   making envelopes, pads, paper bags, cardboard tubes and similar articles in which there is little or no printing as such

cool colours   green or blue, or colours that are predominantly green or blue

coordinate graph   representation of relation between two (sometimes three) variable quantities by plotting series of points (usually joined) along axes known as coordinates:

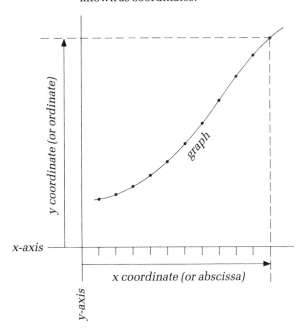

49

COP	initials of *c*entre *o*f *p*rojection: synonym of 'station point' →, commonly used in computer graphics 3D systems
copperplate printing	short-run 'intaglio' → process whereby polished plate is lightly etched so as to carry ink, characterized by sharpness of image, intensity of blacks and slight raised effect; used for visiting and invitation cards
copy	either typewritten matter for typesetting, or all matter intended for reproduction, depending on context
copy camera	see 'process camera'
copy preparation	marking up copy that is to be typeset or reproduced with suitable instructions to operator
copyboard	framed surface onto which original or 'copy' → to be photographed for reproduction is placed
copyfitting	same as 'casting-off' →
copyholder	proof reader who reads aloud from original copy while another checks proof
copy editor	US term for one who sub-edits copy (known in UK as 'sub-editor')
copyright	see 'Universal Copyright Convention 1952'
copytaster	one who selects items for possible inclusion in newspaper
CORA V	acronym for *C*omputer *O*riented *R*eproducer *A*ssembly version *V* (five): Linotype's computer language for controlling 'photocomposition' →
core memory (computers)	old term for internal data store of computer
corner marks	'trim marks' → on artwork, indicating corners for trimming:

corporate identity	same as 'house style' → but sounds posher
corps douze	French equivalent of '12pt' as body size of type (see also 'cicero')
correspondence quality	same as 'letter quality' →

corrigendum (pl: corrigenda)	Latin for 'thing to be corrected'; used to describe item or items corrected subsequent to printing of main part of book
counter	space enclosed by closed parts of type characters such as a b d e g o:

counting keyboard	in photocomposition, input device which keeps tally of operator's position in line, thus requiring him/her to make 'end-of-line' decisions →, as distinct from 'non-counting' keyboard
cover	any paper, board or other material made up to form outside of book
coving	in studio photography, curved background which has no edges or corners between walls and floor
CPA	initials of 'critical path analysis', method of approaching task by using arrow diagram that sets out planning, analysis, scheduling and control functions in clear sequences:

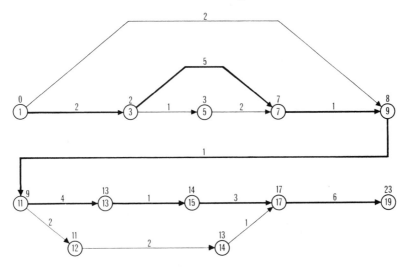

cpi	initials of 'characters per inch'; measure of information that can be accommodated on magnetic tape or drum
CP/M	initials of Control Program/Microcomputers, popular operating system for microcomputers
CPM	initials of 'critical path method'; same as 'CPA' →
cps	initials of 'characters per second'; rate at which machine such as 'teleprinter' → will operate (range is from 12–120cps)

CPU	initials of 'central *p*rocessor *u*nit'; that part of computer comprising main memory, control unit and arithmetic unit
crash	in book binding, strip of muslin used to line spine of book, covering exposed back folds of sections/signatures
crash (computers)	breakdown of system
crash finish	paper finish imparting coarse, linen-like look and feel
crease	to impress paper or board so that it may be more easily folded; same as 'scoring'
creep	movement of blanket on 'blanket cylinder' → during printing, resulting in blurred image
Cromalin	trade name for popular make of 'dry colour proof' →
crop, cropmark, cropping	lines drawn on overlay to show printer which part of photograph is to be used for printed image; see also 'scaling'
cross front	in photography, facility in camera that allows lens to be moved laterally in relation to film, in similar fashion to 'rising front' →
cross-line screen	same as 'halftone screen' (see 'halftone process')
cross-stemmed 'W'	one like this:

cross symbols	some types of cross symbols are:

manx celtic greek latin egyptian St Anthony St Andrews saltire swastika fylfot

patriarchal papal St George maltese Lorraine

crosshead	sub-heading located between paragraphs of text matter in periodical or newspaper; equivalent to 'sub-heading' in book parlance

crown   see 'paper sizes'

CRT   abbreviation for 'cathode *ray* tube'; standard display device in electronic information-handling system, producing visible image on phosphor screen by directed beam of electrons:

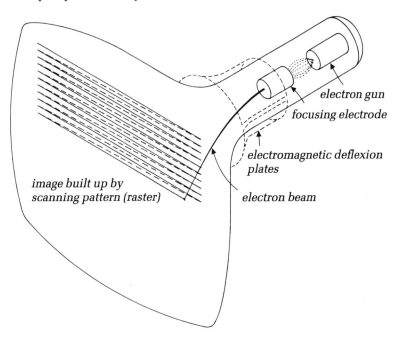

electron gun

focusing electrode

electromagnetic deflexion plates

image built up by scanning pattern (raster)

electron beam

crystal ball   another name for 'rolling-ball' → or 'trackball'
(computers)

CSD   initials of *C*hartered *S*ociety of *D*esigners (UK); known until 1987 as Society of International Artists and Designers (see 'SIAD')

CSG   initials of *c*onstructive *s*olid *g*eometry, one of main techniques in
(computer graphics)   solid modelling of complex screen display images

CSO   initials of '*c*olour *s*eparation *o*verlay' →

cuneiform   wedge-shaped, hence applied to writing of ancient inscriptions on clay tablets:

cursive   used of typeface resembling handwriting, particularly one developed from 'chancery italic' →; see also 'script'

cursor (computers)	moving spot, cross or other symbol showing operator next input point on display; more accurately 'screen cursor' to distinguish from 'hand cursor' →
cut	contraction of 'woodcut', later applied to any illustration from relief printing plate or block; now common in US as synonym for 'block'
cut-and-paste (computer graphics)	interactive method for moving elements in screen display to new location
cut flush	book cover that is trimmed flush with leaves
cut-in-note	one that is set into text matter, thus:
cut-off	standard length – corresponding to that of printing surface for which machine is designed – to which paper is cut on 'web-fed' → press
cut-out (halftone)	another name for 'silhouette halftone' →
cut-out animation	in film animation, technique in which flat, cut-out shapes, sometimes with articulated joints, are moved manually between single stop-frame exposures
cutaway shot	in cinefilm and TV, one away from main action, often used to cover for omitted part of action (see also 'reaction shot')
cutline	US term for caption under an illustration (cut = letterpress block)
cutting-and-creasing press	'die-cutting' → press which includes blunt blades for creasing as well as sharp blades for cutting
cutting copy	in cinefilm, print used for editing, usually from 'rushes', and from which is produced first 'rough-cut', then 'fine-cut' copy; called 'workprint' in US
CWP (computers)	initials of *c*ommunicating *w*ord *p*rocessor →
cyan	blue/green colour containing no red; one of three primaries used in 'subtractive colour mixing' →
cybernetics	study of control, communication and self-correction in mechanisms
cyclorama	curved cloth or paper background used in studio photography
cylinder press	printing machine using impression cylinder, as distinct from 'platen press':

cylindrical projections

group of projections of Earth in which plane of projection is cylinder assumed to touch globe along one parallel (usually equator):

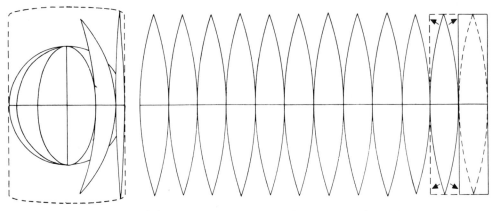

globe is segmented and segments are straightened out, remaining joined only at equator; segments are then converted into rectangles so that they adjoin along their whole length

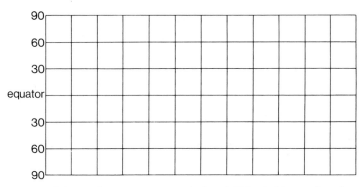

plate carrée: areas exaggerated and distorted towards poles

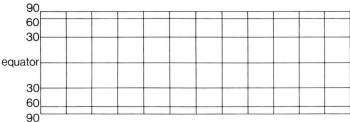

equal area orthographic: areas equal but badly distorted towards poles

continued overleaf

continued

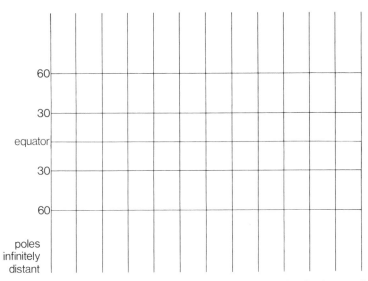

60
30
equator
30
60
poles
infinitely
distant

Mercator's suitable only for navigation; hopelessly distorted land masses

Cyrillic alphabet used throughout USSR; descended from Greek, devised in 9th century to incorporate characters expressing sounds peculiar to Slav tongue; not used for printing types until 18th century:

абгдезхуиклмнјопрњстsЬцв
АБГДЕЗХУИКЛМНЈОПРСТSФЦЦВ

D

dagger type character used as second order of 'reference marks' → in footnotes; sometimes called 'obelisk' or 'long cross'

daisy wheel printer typewriter or other 'impact printer' → employing flat, circular typing element known as 'daisy wheel'; on which type characters are positioned at ends of spokes; much used in 'word processor' → systems:

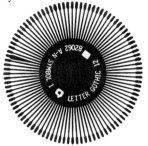

56

dandy roll	cylinder of wire gauze on papermaking machine that imparts pattern of wiremarks onto paper
dark trace CRT	'CRT' → in which electron beam makes dark image against white surface of tube
data	factual information; used in data processing, especially of information held in memory store of computer; though properly plural (singular: datum) many authorities now treat 'data' as singular collective noun
data bank (computers)	comprehensive data file stored in computer: expression not much used in practice
data base (computers)	large store of digitized information organized so that all users draw on one common body of knowledge, eg: World Patent Index, typically accessed by combinations of 'keywords' →
data capture (computers)	general term embracing all methods of converting data to machine-readable form
data carrier (computers)	in data processing, any medium, such as magnetic tape or paper tape, used for recording data
data compression (computers)	technique of shortening transmission time for data transfer
data link (computers)	any channel, such as telephone, used to connect remote parts of system
data matrix	array of quantities set out in columns and rows, representing variables and values they may take
data phone, data set	same as 'modem' →
data processing (computers)	handling of information in mechanical, electromechanical and – most typically – electronic systems
data sink (computers)	slang for any terminal, or part of terminal, that accepts input data
data tablet (computer graphics)	same as 'digitizing pad', 'tablet' and 'bit pad'
Datavision	name of Swedish 'videotex' system
date line	line of type at head of newspaper item, giving day, date and place of origin of news item if not local
datum	known or given fact (singular of 'data')
Day-Glo	brand name of popular make of fluorescent pigment mainly used in screen printing

daylight film	colour film for use in daylight, fluorescent light or flashlight
De Stijl	Dutch for 'The Style'; art and design movement originating in Netherlands in 1917, advocating principles (eg: asymmetry, use of primary colours, emphasis on rectilinear forms) which have had immense influence on development of graphic design
dead matter (type)	set matter no longer intended for use, as distinct from 'live matter'
dead metal	non-printing areas in letterpress engraving
debug (computers)	correct error in system
decal	printed transfer with adhesive back, now usually made in plastics
deckle edge	ragged edge of handmade paper, sometimes simulated on machine-made paper
dedicated	said of program, system or routine constructed or set aside for particular purpose
deep-etch plate	lithographic plate made from photographic positive as distinct from albumen plate →; image is slightly recessed below surface of plate, allowing thicker film of ink to be carried in recesses and permitting longer print runs
deep-etched halftone	letterpress plate of screened halftone subject, in which additional etching is carried out to eliminate halftone dot completely in selected areas
degradation	tendency of transmitted signals, eg: video display, to deteriorate
dejagging (computer graphics)	same as 'anti-aliasing' →
delete	proof instruction to remove letter, word, phrase, sentence or paragraph crossed through, indicated by symbol:

too̸ much   ᵹ

denominator	number below or behind line in vulgar fraction; other number is 'nominator':

$$\frac{1}{3} \qquad \tfrac{1}{3}$$

densitometer	optical instrument that measures intensity of colour or tone on opaque or transparent subject matter
depth of field	in photography, zone of acceptable sharpness in front of and behind a subject on which camera is focused; depth of field is affected by

relative distance of object from camera, 'focal length' → of lens, and aperture → of lens:

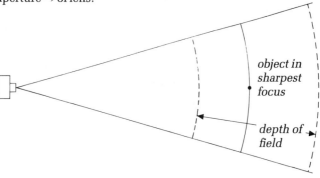

depth of field at f2.8   stopped down to f11

depth of focus   in photography, range of position of film in relation to lens, in which acceptably sharp focus can be obtained:

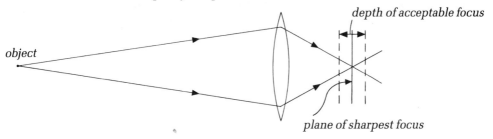

descender   that part of certain lower-case letters, such as g p q y appearing below 'x-height' →

descender line   imaginary horizontal line connecting bottoms of descender letters

59

descriptor	letter, word, number or other sign used to identify or describe
design assistant	1) one who does work for which senior designer takes credit 2) one who claims to know more about design in six weeks than senior designer has learned in sixteen years
Design Council	State sponsored body founded 1944 as Council of Industrial Design to promote cause of 'good' (?) design in British Industry but sadly crippled by dependence on financial support from industry
desktop computer	same as 'microcomputer' →
desktop publishing	system involving use of 'personal computer' → with software controlling 'word processor' →, 'page make-up' → and (optionally) 'laser printer' → permitting full control of operation by originator of text
detail paper	thin, hard, semi-transparent paper used for sketches and layouts
device coordinates (computer graphics)	those representing any part of display that is keyed to x–y coordinate system
device independent (computers)	program or language that may be run on variety of machines
Dewey Decimal Classification	devised by Melvil Dewey in 1876 to classify areas of knowledge, divided into ten main, numbered classes (eg: philosophy = 100) and sub-divided progressively into ten sub-classes, each of which is divided into ten sub-sub-classes, and so on; still in use (in modified form) in libraries all over the world (see also 'UDC')
dia-	prefix meaning 'through', 'apart' or 'across'
diacritical mark/sign	one used to differentiate sounds or values of character; see 'accented (diacritical) signs'
diaeresis	see 'accented (diacritical) signs'
diagonal fraction	one like this: ⅓, as distinct from one like this: $\frac{1}{3}$
diagonal scale	method by which existing scale may be used to derive another by extending parallels, thus:

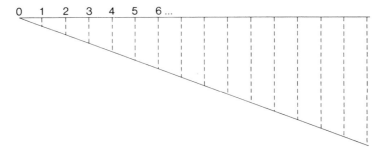

dialup (computers)	dialling special number to access computer via standard telephone network
diaphragm (of camera)	see 'aperture'
diapositive	positive photographic transparency
diascope	projector of transparent subject matter such as diapositives or slides; also called 'slide projector' (but see also 'overhead projector')
diazo	limited-quantity reproduction process in which transparent or translucent original exposed to light source produces image on light-sensitive material (paper, cloth or film), which is developed by liquid, ammonia vapour or heat; prints can be black, blue or other colours (abbreviation of 'diazonium')
Didon	name of French 'teletext', ie: broadcast 'videotex' → system
didones	British Standards term for those typefaces otherwise known as 'moderns' (see 'type classification')
Didot point	typographic measurement system established in 1775 by French typefounder François Didot, now used in most European countries as alternative to Anglo-American point system; Didot point is now accepted as 0.375mm (0.0148in)
die-cutting	cutting paper or board by means of steel blades made up on forme; used in packaging and display work
die-stamping	stamping out raised, usually coloured, impression on paper or board by means of matched dies
digipad	abbreviated form of 'digitizing pad' →
digital camera	one that records images in digital form, used as input device for computer-controlled graphic information system
digital computer	one which operates on information presented to it in binary digits, to make calculations of the kind required in, for example, photocomposition
digital dial	one in which data are represented by discrete set of numbers, as contrasted with 'analog dial' →
digital painting system (computer graphics)	'raster scan display process system' → devoted to constructing broadcast television images to 525 line (US) or 625 line (European) standards, either from scratch or by adapting existing picture; high resolution systems (at least 2000 lines) now permit more delicate results
digital plotter (computers)	same as 'graph plotter' →

digital-to-analog converter (computers)   one that converts data in digital form into analog form

digitize   to render image into coded signal which can be processed electronically and used to reconstruct image in digitized form; images may be prepared in advance for electronic processing, or modified during scanning:

  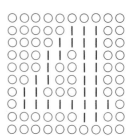

non-digitized numerals superimposed on grid   *gridded numerals as recognized by scanner*   *digital numerals as stored for retrieval*

digitizing pad (computers)   input device on-line to digital computer, on which free-hand drawing is translated almost immediately into digitized form visible on linked CRT; also known as 'tablet':

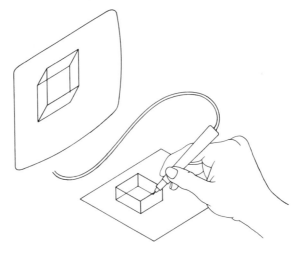

digram, digraph	group of two letters which represent one sound, as in 'ph' of digra*ph*
dimensioning	to avoid confusion, terms used in dimensioning representations of three-dimensional objects are: 'length', 'width', 'height'; 'depth' is not recommended
dimetric projection	see 'axonometric projections'
DIN	initials of *D*eutsche *I*ndustrie *N*orm: standard published by the German standards institution, which gave birth to the DIN (now ISO) paper size standards and to the DIN film speed ratings
dingbat	type ornament such as star, flash, fist or bullet (US term)
dinky-dash	same as 'jim-dash' →; more common in US
diphthong	union of two vowels pronounced in one syllable, as in 'loud', 'coil'; commonly used to describe 'ligature' → of two vowels, as in 'æ', 'œ', though these should more properly be called 'monophthongs'
direct accessing (computers)	retrieving 'record' → by means of 'address' without necessity of serial search
direct data entry (computers)	keying-in to computer without intermediate step such as making punched cards
direct display (computers)	VDU that is employed to display data in alphanumeric or graphic form direct from computer's 'memory' →
direct-entry	system combining input, output and computer, in which type is set as copy is keyed in
direct image master	short-run litho plate, usually made from paper (hence 'paper plate') or plastic which is typed on directly
direct impression	form of type composition using typewriter; also known as 'typewriter composition', 'strike-on composition' and 'cold composition'
direct view storage tube	see 'DVST'
directory (computers)	catalogue comprising all names and locations stored on disk or tape
dirty copy	manuscript or typescript for typesetting that contains many corrections
dirty proof	one containing many errors or corrections
discretionary hyphen	in photocomposition, one inserted by operator into polysyllabic word to show machine most suitable position for word-break if type line justification requires; automatically removed if not relevant

63

disk (matrix)	in photocomposition, an image-carrier in disk form
disk, disc (computers)	see 'magnetic disk'
diskette (computers)	same as 'floppy disk' →
display background (VDU)	section of displayed image that cannot be changed by operator
display list (computer graphics)	instructions containing data required to specify items that may be drawn on display
display matter	any type matter not part of body of the text
display processing unit	see 'DPU'
display size	any size of type above 14pt, as distinct from 'text size' or 'composition size'
display surface (computer graphics)	any output device that displays graphical data, such as 'VDU' → or 'graph plotter' →
dissolve	in cinefilm and TV, 'fade-in' superimposed on 'fade-out' →
distribute, dis, diss	to break up composed type and melt it down or return it to case
ditto marks	signs used to indicate repeat of what is on line above, thus: .. .. ..
dittogram/dittograph	repeated letter within word, caused by typesetting error
divided circle	see 'pie graph'
DL	envelope size in ISO Series of 110 × 220mm; will conveniently accommodate A4 sheet folded twice on long edge to 99 × 210mm:

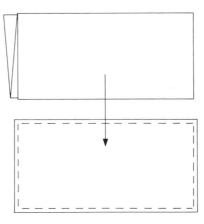

docfax	jargon for 'facsimile transmission' → of documents

doctor blade	in photogravure, flexible metal blade that scrapes excess ink from surface of plate or cylinder before printing, leaving ink only in 'cells'
documentary	term coined in late 1920s by Scottish film maker John Grierson to describe work of American film maker Robert Flaherty, which focused on real people engaged in real-life tasks and pursuits, and containing a large measure of social concern; later extended to include similar work in still photography
dodging	in photography, controlling exposure in printing by partial masking of selected portion of print under enlarger
dog's cock	printer's slang for exclamation mark
dolly shot	in cinefilm and TV, one made with camera mounted on special wheeled truck
dongle (computers)	in computer-driven photocomposition, device implanted to prevent unauthorized transfer of software or type founts from one machine to another (see also 'mumping')
dope sheet	in cinefilm and TV graphics, chart listing order of cels, etc, against sequence of shots, instructions for panning, tracking, zooming, mixing or fading, and time required for these; more commonly known in US as 'exposure sheet'
DOR	initials of *d*igital *o*ptical *r*ecording: technique using 'optical digital disk' → to record digital information
DOS (computers)	initials of *d*isk *o*perating *s*ystem: one installed to regulate access and use of disks
dot-dot-dot (as spoken)	verbal identification of 'ellipsis' →
dot-for-dot reproduction	making line facsimile from existing screened image of continuous tone subject, for further reproduction without re-screening
dot gain	tendency for dots of 'halftone screen' → to swell during stages of photomechanical process; needs to be compensated for
dot matrix	generally, any array from which pattern of dots may be selected to form image, specifically, one used as basis for character formation in 'matrix printer' →
double-black duotone	'duotone' → in which both plates are printed black
double-burning	US term for combining two or more film positives → or negatives as one for photomechanical reproduction; also known as 'surprinting' and in UK as 'stripping up as one'
double coated paper	one that has been given two applications of china clay to produce high quality finish

65

double dagger	type character used as third order of 'reference marks' →; also known as 'diesis' or 'double obelisk'
double-dot halftone	'duotone' →, especially one in which both impressions are in same colour
double-headed	in cinefilm, running separate picture and sound track simultaneously on editing machine or projector, to judge effect before transcribing sound onto 'optical track' →
double spread	any left- and right-hand pair of pages in book or periodical; may be 'centre spread' → or 'false double' →
doubling	in printing, defect in machine function causing inked image to be printed twice
down (computers)	said of computer that is out of action, usually due to fault, or for maintenance
download (computers)	transfer data or program from one computer to another
downloadable typeface	in photocomposition, one stored in supplier's host computer and transferred to printer as required
downstroke (of type)	heavy stroke in type character, derived from downward movement of pen in calligraphy:

downtime (computers)	time lapse during which computer and/or 'ts peripherals are out of action due to fault or maintenance work
DP	initials of *data processing*
DPE (computer graphics)	initials of *Digital Production Effects*, system developed in UK by Quantel to manipulate moving images by altering size, constructing inserts, rotating, inverting and distorting on command; fore-runner to the 'Quantel Paintbox' →
DPI, dpi	initials of *dots per inch*
DPU	initials of *display processing unit*: special-purpose 'CPU' → devised to execute sequence of display functions in 'random-scan' → or 'raster-scan' → mode
dragging (computer graphics)	repositioning image on display screen by interactive technique

drawing-on cover	attaching cover to paperback or periodical by glueing to spine and to part of end leaves (see also 'wrappering cover')
dressing	packing cylinder of printing press to modify impression and improve printed result
driography	same as 'letterset' →
driver program (computers)	one used in 'front-end system' → to control access to machine's routines
driving out	spacing words to fill line of type; widely practised in times past by printers because they were paid by number of lines set
drop	space left by design between top of maximum type area and first line of main body of text (see also 'chapter drop')
drop cap	in typesetting, initial at beginning of text which is set in larger size of type, extending into lines of type below:

HOWEVER carefully the arrangement of solidl
matter may have been planned, with referenc
size and measure, for example, and however
that matter is subsequently set, it can almost always

drop-down	same as 'chapter drop' →
drop out	elimination, by whatever means, of some part of image so that it will not print (see also 'drop(ped)-out halftone'); also used, especially in US, as synonym for 'save out' →
drop out blue	any marker (usually blue crayon) used to write specifications on 'camera-ready artwork' → which will not be 'seen' by process camera and so will not be reproduced
drop(ped)-out halftone	one in which halftone dot has been eliminated from highlight areas to give more brilliant result; also known as 'highlight halftone'
drop-tone, drop-out	same as 'line conversion' →
dropped head	page heading that is positioned below upper limit of type area
dropped initial	same as 'drop-cap' →
drum (matrix)	in photocomposition, an 'image-carrier' → in drum form
drum plotter (computers)	output device in which writing tool moves laterally across width of roll of paper which is at same time being rotated on drum, thus permitting reasonably accurate reproduction of drawings, though not as good as 'flat-bed plotter' →

drum printer (computer graphics)	same as 'barrel printer' (see 'computer output devices')
dry-based ink	one in which colour is derived from aniline dye
dry colour proof	any not requiring manufacture of printing plates as preliminary to proofing
dry litho plate	one that does not need damping in preparation for taking an impression
dry offset	same as 'letterset' →
dry-processing	technique of photographic processing that does not involve dunking photosensitive material in liquid; highly suited to computer-generated imaging
dry transfer	see 'transfer lettering'
DTP	initials of '*desk top publishing*' →
DTR	initials of *diffusion-transfer-reversal*: reprographic process which produces both negative and positive copy in single processing step; also known as 'chemical transfer'
duck-foot quotes	another name for '*guillemets*' →
dummy	sample made up to show format, substance and bulk of intended publication; may also include some graphic representation of print matter, thus forming 'presentation visual' →
dump (computers)	to transfer data from one part of system to another
duotone	matched set of two halftones, each of same subject but with different 'screen angles' →; varying effects can be got by making one halftone more contrasty than its mate (sometimes called 'duograph')
dupe	slang for duplicate
duplex	any device (usually electronic) capable of transmitting or receiving signals in either direction simultaneously
duplex board	one consisting of two layers of different colour and/or quality, pasted together
duplex halftone	same as duotone, now less used
duplex mould	one used to hold two character matrices on typecasting machines
duplicator paper	soft, absorbent material for use with duplicating machine
dust wrapper/jacket	same as 'book jacket' →

DVST (computer graphics)	initials of *direct-view storage tube*: device similar to 'CRT' →, except that displayed image does not have to be refreshed, is flicker-free and has very high resolution, but is much slower in changing image
dye transfer print	photographic colour print of high quality made from either opaque colour original via film 'interneg' → or from negative colour transparency; suitable for photomechanical reproduction and for one-off display prints
dyeline	same as 'diazo' →

E

E13B	character set – consisting only of numerals and some signs – specially designed for 'MICR' →
EAN	initials of *European Article Number*; one of two most prevalent 'bar codes' →; other is Universal Product Code (US) →
ear (of newspaper)	small display element on either side of newspaper 'nameplate' →
ear (of type)	small projection at top right of lower-case g:

early copies	same as 'advance copies' →
easel binder	one which is constructed so that contents can be displayed:

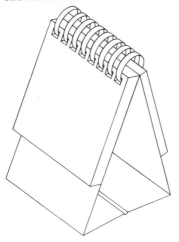

EBCDIC (computers)	initials of *Extended Binary Coded Decimal Interchange Code*; one devised by IBM, giving 256 possible character positions

ECPS   initials of *e*lectronic *c*olour *p*re-press *s*ystem

edge-notched card   hand-sorting, coordinate indexing system in which holes along one
index   or more edges of file card are given coded meaning; some holes are
                        converted into notches by clipping away that part of card between
                        card edge and hole, so that, when needle or rod is inserted into pack
                        of cards and raised, notched cards are left below:

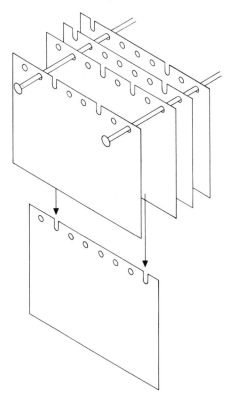

editing machine   in cinefilm, one on which film can be run at projection speed,
                        together with one or more separate sound tracks; also allows editor to
                        stop or reverse run and allows easy access to film for cutting

editing terminal   device using cathode ray tube (CRT) to display and correct
                        keyboarded input in tape-stored photocomposition before printing
                        out

edition   complete output of publication from one set of printing formes,
                        whether in one impression or several; 'new edition' implies some
                        change in content and/or style of production

edition-bound   same as 'cased' or 'case-bound' →; US term not so common in UK

EDP   initials of *e*lectronic *d*ata *p*rocessing

eg   initials of *exempli gratia*, Latin for 'for example'

egyptian	name at first applied to both sans-serif and slab-serif typefaces by early 19th-century founders, later reserved for slab-serifs; also known as 'antique'
eight-sheet	poster size 60 × 80in (153 × 203cm)
EL	initials of *eye level* (see 'perspective projections')
electromagnetic spectrum	complete series of those wave forms which travel through space at speed of light; visible spectrum is one portion of this:

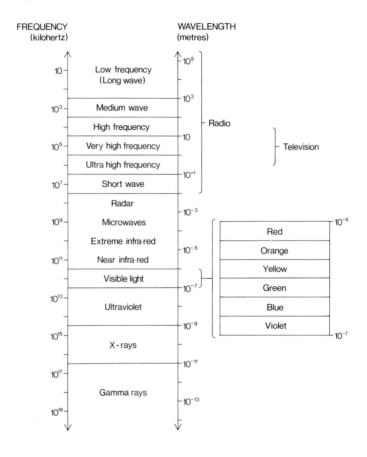

electronic drawing board (computers)	combination of CRT and 'graphic tablet' →
electronic mail	use of electronic transmission devices – 'telex' →, 'facsimile' →, 'word-processor' →, 'modem' → – to convey data, text matter and pictures instantaneously all over the world; abbreviated as 'EM'
electronic page scanning	'scanner' → having capacity to scan separate parts of page including text matter, line artwork, black and white halftone subjects and colour transparencies, then produce complete film assembly

electronic retouching (computer graphics)	manipulation of scanned image before viewing, broadcasting or publication by enlarging 'pixel' → size of portion of image to modify colour or intensity
electrophotographic printing	any process involving use of electrical signals in combination with photosensitive material; most significant form is 'laser printing' →
electrostatic printer	one in which electrostatic charge is applied to those parts of paper that are to be printed, attracting fine powder which is then fixed by application of heat
electrostatic processes	those involving phenonemon of static electricity (see 'xerography')
electrotype, electro	duplicate letterpress plate made from an original plate by electroplating process
elite (typewriter)	smaller of two commonest 'typewriter faces' →
ellipse	in practical terms, any oblique view of circle, but see 'conic sections', also 'super ellipse':
ellipsis	sign used to indicate that something has been left out of phrase or sentence, thus . . .
elliptical dot screen	form of screen used in 'halftone screen' → using elliptical, as against halftone dot pattern
EM	abbreviation for '*electronic m*ail' →
em	in typesetting, dimension derived from square of any given type size, so that 8pt em is 8pts × 8pts, and so on; width of type lines, type areas, etc are traditionally given in 'pica ems' →
em-quad	type space that is square of type size; colloquially known as 'mutton' →
em-rule/dash	one used to indicate omission of word, or – by some – to open and close parenthetical phrase, as alternative to spaced 'en-rule' →
embossing	producing raised impression on board or paper, usually by 'die-stamping' →
emulation (computers)	use of hardware or program to make one system perform with characteristics of another system
emulsion	essential light-sensitive coating on photographic materials; 'emulsion-side' of film is the dull one that faces lens (and therefore subject of photograph)
emulsion side up/down	important factor in 'photomechanical process' →, which must be agreed in advance between process film maker and printer since it affects choice between 'wrong-reading' image on emulsion (that is,

reversed left-to-right) or 'right-reading' image

en — half the width of an em →; as average width of a type character, it is useful unit for costing and copyfitting calculation

en-quad — type space half width of 'em-quad' →; colloquially known as 'nut' →

en-rule/dash — one used to denote 'and' as in 'man–machine interface', 'to' as in 'Paris–London flight' or – when spaced – to open and close parenthetical phrase', though some, especially in US, prefer an 'em-rule/dash' → for this purpose

enamel paper — one-sided, highly finished coated paper used for box covers and colour proofing

end even — instruction to compositor: end 'take' → on full line

end-matter (of book) — those parts of book that follow main body of text, more correctly (but less commonly) called 'subsidiaries', also (in US) 'back matter' and 'postlims'; following sequence is offered as reasonable but not immutable:

appendices	acknowledgements (or could be in prelims)
author's notes	index
glossary	imprint (more usually in prelims)
bibliography	

end-of-line decisions — in type composition, those decisions that must be made at end of line of text in regard to justification and word-breaks; traditionally such decisions were made by compositor but it is now possible to program computer to make many of them

endoscope — see 'fibre optics'

endpapers — sheets at each end of cased book that are used to fasten leaves to cover; also known as 'endleaves' or (in US) 'endsheets'

endpoints (computer graphics) — in 'vector display' →, those at each end of 'line segment' →

EOM (computers) — initials of end-of-message, used to terminate message

EOR (computers) — initials of end-of-run or end-of-record

EOT (computers) — initials of end-of-transmission

EPCS — initials of electronic page composition system

epidiascope — projector for either transparent or opaque subject matter

episcope — projector for opaque subject matter such as pages of book

EPROM (computers) — acronym for erasable programmable read-only memory: one that can be re-used by removing it, erasing and rewriting all or part of its contents, and replacing it in the computer (see also 'ROM' and 'PROM')

ergonomics study of people in their working environments in relation to design of machine controls, work spaces and methods, information devices and all such factors affecting efficiency, comfort and health

erratum (pl: errata) item omitted from publication, acknowledged by subsequent inclusion of erratum/errata slip

escapement in photocomposition, device controlling movement of system, whether optical or electronic

eszett German language character representing 'ss':

ß

et seq abbreviation for *et sequens*, Latin for 'and the following'

etaoin shrdlu in typesetting, letters on first two vertical rows of keys on Linotype and other linecasting machines; used by typesetter to indicate that line will be reset or discarded

etching harnessing of chemical effect of acid on metal to produce printable image

eth Old English character representing 'th' as in 'those':

ð

Euler circle see 'Venn diagram'

Euronet communications network linking European countries under aegis of European Economic Commission

even page one having even page number, that is, lefthand page

even word spacing same as 'fixed word spacing' →

even working piece of print that is contained in sections of 16, 32, 48 or 64 pages, with no need for odd 4 or 8 page section

event (computers) any operator-initiated action such as keying-in or manipulating 'stylus' → or 'mouse' →

exception dictionary in computer-aided photocomposition, memory store of word-breaks which do not conform to standard pattern

exclusive type area type area of page excluding running headline and page number

exotic (typeface) traditionally applied by European printers to any typeface which does not conform to Latin letter forms, eg: Arabic

| **expanded/extended** | used to describe wider version of normal typeface: |

abcde
ABCD

exposure meter	in photography, device for making light readings to aid calculation of exposure time, employing one of three types of photocell: selenium, cadmium sulphide (CdS) or silicon blue
exposure sheet	in film animation, US term for 'dope sheet' →
extent (computer graphics)	notional line or rectangle separating or enclosing segment of display
extremes	in film animation, drawings made at significant points in movements of animated subjects; also known as 'keys' or 'keyframes', especially in US:

extreme

in-betweens

in-betweens

extreme

75

extrusion (computer graphics)	modelling technique whereby line may be drawn from established point, line or plane
eyebrow	same as 'strap' →; more common in US
eye-legible copy	used of microform record that contains title or other lettering legible to naked eye

F

f-number, f stop	see 'aperture'
face	printing surface of type; also, design of type, hence 'typeface'
face/fade out blue	synonym for 'drop-out blue' →
facetted classification	system of identifying elements in collection of information – such as book – so that they can be compared with elements defined by person seeking information, as distinct from less flexible systems such as 'Dewey' → or 'UDC' →; very suited to punched-card or edge-notched card sorting
facetting (computer graphics)	in modelling display, construction of 'polygon mesh' →
facsimile, facsim	exact copy, especially of manuscript, print matter or work of art, with no reduction or enlargement
facsimile compressor	form of 'facsimile transmission' → that allows continuous tone picture to be transmitted in seconds rather than minutes
facsimile laser platemaker	facsimile transmission device that makes printing plate directly from transmitted image, by means of laser
facsimile transmission	system that sends representation of document over telecommunication link in form that is accurate to original, not merely a version of content; typically makes use of electronic scanning technique, originally analog, now increasingly digital
fade-in, fade-out	in cinefilm and TV, changing from black to picture (fade-in) or picture to black (fade-out)
fade-out halftone	synonym for 'vignetted halftone' →
false double	'double spread' → in which printed image cannot extend over continuous surface as on 'centre spread' → but must be split when printing

family (typeface)   complete range of design variants of particular typeface:

abcd abcd **abcd** *abcd*
ABC ABC **ABC** *ABC*

abcd abcd abcd
ABC ABC ABC

abcd abcd
ABC ABC

fan-fold   mechanical folding method for continuous stationery

fart box (computers)   slang for 'text retrieval terminal' →

fast emulsion   in photography, one needing less exposure

fat face   roman typeface in which contrast between thick and thin strokes is very marked, eg:

ABCabc

fat matter   printer's slang for copy that can be set quickly because it includes a lot of space (eg: dialogue in novels); opposite of 'lean matter'

fax   slang for electronically transmitted images produced by scanning original (from 'facsimile' →)

FCC   initials of *F*ederal *C*ommunications *C*ommission, US government authority responsible for telecommunications

FDW   initials of '*f*ree *d*elivery to (customer's) *w*arehouse': stated on specifications and quotations for print

feature card index   see 'peek-a-boo card index'

feedback   in electronic transmission, return of some part of output of system to input, positive feedback re-inforcing input, negative feedback reducing it; in information sciences generally, negative feedback forms essential element of self-correcting control systems

feeder mechanism on any 'sheet-fed' → printing machine that transfers sheets from stack of paper onto machine proper

feint lines typical product of 'run-through work' →: horizontal and/or vertical lines (customarily light blue) ruled on sheets which are made up as manuscript books and account books

felt-side that side of uncoated paper away from 'wire-side' →

Fibonacci series number series discovered by Leonardo of Pisa (nicknamed Fibonacci) in 12th century, in which each number is sum of two preceding numbers, thus: 1 2 3 5 8 13 21 34 55 . . .

fibre optics technique of transmitting image through flexible bundle of fine, tubular fibres, allowing subjects in narrow confines to be examined and/or photographed by means of device called an 'endoscope'

field in broadcast television, video and any other form of 'raster scan' →, area covered by one complete scan of display screen

field area/size in cinefilm and TV, area viewed by camera from any given position:

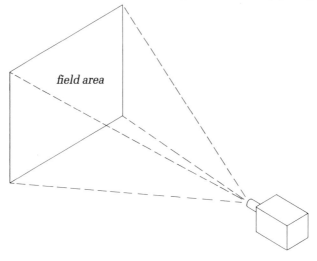

field area

field guide specially printed sheet on which 'zooming' and 'panning' movements are planned in film animation

fifth-generation computer one that is designed to be addressed in ordinary language and that performs operations resembling human capacity for learning and decision-making, ie: 'artificial intelligence'

figure (in book) traditional term for line illustration incorporated within text pages of book, as distinct from 'plate' →; often abbreviated as 'fig' (pl: 'figs')

figure (type) term commonly used by printers and typefounders for 'numeral'

file (computers) structured collection of 'records' → that have some common source or purpose, housed in magnetic disk, tape or drum

fill character   one added to 'character set' → to make it up to required number

fill pattern
(computer graphics)   selection of patterns and tones offered by most computer graphics packages

filling-in   printing fault resulting in filling in of 'counters' → of type and of fine white dots in halftones

film-advance   in photocomposition, amount by which sensitive material in 'photo-unit' → is advanced to achieve required distance between lines of output

film animation   in cinefilm and TV, shooting of separate film frames in sequence to produce illusion of movement; any shot which is not achieved by conventional photography at constant camera speed will involve some measure of film animation, though most common uses are for cartoons and title/credit sequences

film assembly   in photolithography, assembly of film negatives or positives in position for making printing plates

film composition   inaccurate and ambiguous synonym for 'photocomposition' →

film mechanical   same as 'film assembly' →

**film negative/
positive**   any transparent substrate carrying image, whether positive or negative, used in 'photomechanical process' →

film sizes   commonly available sizes of film for use in still cameras are:

110   16mm film width, perforated one side; twelve or twenty exposures 13 × 17mm in cartridge

126   35mm film width, perforated one side; twelve or twenty exposures 26 × 26mm in cartridge

135   35mm film width, perforated both sides; forty or seventy-two exposures 18 × 24mm in cassette, twelve, twenty or thirty-six exposures 24 × 36mm in cassette

120   62mm film width, in unperforated roll with backing paper; fifteen exposures 45 × 60mm, twelve exposures 60 × 60mm, ten exposures 60 × 70mm, eight exposures 60 × 90mm

220   62mm film width, in unperforated roll without backing paper; same range of image sizes as for 120, but with double number of exposures in each

sheet film comes in large variety of sizes of which common traditional ones are:

quarter-plate 83 × 108mm (3¼ × 4¾in)*
halfplate 121 × 165mm (4¾ × 6½in)*
whole-plate 165 × 216mm (6½ × 8½in)*
203 × 254mm (8 × 10in)
102 × 127mm (4 × 5in)
* now obsolescent and being replaced by 'A' sizes

film speed	all photographic film – including cinefilm – has a speed rating (the higher the number, the faster the film) from which is calculated exposure; two matching standards, ASA and DIN, are used, and these are shown on calibration scales of exposure meters, film speed dials on cameras, and film containers, where both ASA and DIN are incorporated under 'ISO' → label
film strip (matrix)	in photocomposition, 'image-carrier' → in form of film strip
filmograph	in film animation; technique whereby movements of rostrum camera and table create effect of animation from artwork and still photographs
filmsetting	used as synonym for 'photocomposition' → but not so suitable as generic term since it implies setting only on film, for which specific function it is best reserved
filter	in photography, sheet of glass, plastic or gelatin placed between subject and lens of camera, which modifies or eliminates certain colour from emulsion film
filter factor	adjustment which must be made in photographic exposure when filter is used
final film	'film negative/positive' → from which printing plate is made, and which incorporates final corrections
fine screen	any 'halftone screen' → of 100 lines to the inch (40 lines to the centimetre) or finer
finial letter	special sort in some typefaces intended for use only at end of word or line; see 'swash letter'
finish	treatment of paper surface to give final effect, during manufacture or subsequently
finished art	same as 'artwork' →
finished rough	nonsense term for 'presentation visual' →
finishing	any operation following work on printing machine, such as laminating, binding and trimming
firmware	computer programs embodied in components which cannot themselves be altered by user but may be removed and replaced
first and third	sheet or card on which printing appears on both sides of single-fold job, thus needing impression on two sides of sheet as contrasted with 'french fold' →
first angle projection	see 'multiview projections'
first line form advance	in word-processing and photocomposition, automatic advance of printing paper in position for first line of next page

fish-eye lens	one which has an extremely wide angle (about 150°–180°) producing very distorted circular image:

fist	printer's slang for index mark in form of pointing hand:

fit-up halftones	in letterpress, two or more halftone plates which are made separately but fitted up together in mounting, as distinct from 'stripped-up halftones' which are combined at negative stage and made up as one plate
fix, fixer	chemical solution used to make images on photographic film and prints permanent; in slang use, same as 'hypo'
fixed word spacing	typesetting mode in which word spaces are all standard, any extra space being left at end of line, same as 'even word spacing' →; this book is set to fixed word spacing throughout
flag (computers)	addition to item of transmitted data to identify its character or kind, usually in form of distinctive character; also known as 'sentinel' or 'tag'
flag (of newspaper)	same as 'nameplate' →
flange	below-type-height edge of letterpress halftone plate, through which

it is secured to mount by pins; now often unnecessary as plates are adhesive mounted

flap

that part of book jacket which is folded over the boards of the case, front and back, and usually includes description of book

flash-harry

derogatory term applied by some graphic designers to their more imaginative colleagues

flat

in photolitho platemaking, special opaque base from which 'windows' are cut for insertion of negative material, whole assembly forming composite used to print down image on albumen plate; also called 'mask'

flat-back book

synonym for 'square-back book' →

flat-bed cylinder press

printing machine using impression cylinder as distinct from 'platen press' → and having flat printing surface as distinct from 'rotary press' →

flat-bed plotter (computer graphics)

computer output device consisting of flat drawing table traversed by writing-tool assembly which produces drawings on paper or film to high standard of accuracy

flat-bed scanner

one of two types used in 'facsimile transmission' →; other is 'cylinder scanner'

flat colour

printed area of colour with no tonal variation

flat panel displays (computers)

those screen output devices not based on cathode ray tube and thus flatter; most significant are 'LCD' → and 'plasma-panel display' →:

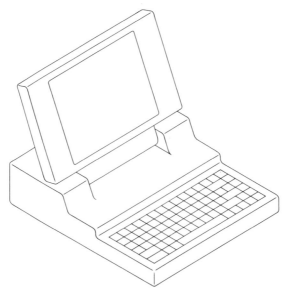

flat plan	diagram setting out page-by-page arrangement of periodical or book; also known, especially in US, as 'thumbnail layout'
flat-tint halftone	matching halftone with flat tint to print under it in separate colour
fleuron	see 'printer's flower'
flexography	relief printing process using curved plates of rubber or soft plastic; used mostly for packaging and paper bags
flier	promotional leaflet or sheet
flip (as verb)	used by some as synonym for 'flop' → but equally ambiguous
flip box	same as 'flop-over box' →
flip-flop	electrical or electronic device that can switch to one or two possible stats (on/off, yes/no, 0/1) on receipt of appropriate signal
flippy (computers)	ambiguous: may refer to double-sided 'floppy disk' →, but may also be straight synonym for floppy disk
flippy-floppy	double-sided version of 'floppy disk' →
floating accent	in typesetting, separate accent mark which can be 'floated' over suitable lower-case character (known as 'piece accent' in US)
floating bar graph	one in which variables occur at either end of bar:

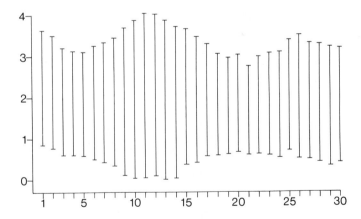

flong	material used for making moulds from type matter, from which stereos → are cast; also called 'matrix' or 'mat'
flop (as verb)	to turn transparent image, such as negative or film positive, so that it is reversed back to front, whether by intention or accident; ambiguous as an instruction, so better replaced by more precise terms 'reverse image left to right', 'reverse image back to front and top to bottom' or 'turn image through 180° top to bottom'

83

flop-over box, flop box	in film animation, device by means of which still image appears to rotate horizontally or vertically:

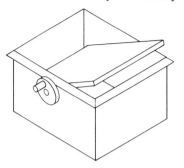

floppy disk (computers)	'magnetic disk' → of flexible plastic, designed to be handled within protecting envelope; used with word-processors and other micro-computers
floppy disk drive (computers)	device for handling one or more 'floppy disks' →, 'reading' them as they rotate on drive shaft
floret	see 'printer's flower'
flourish (type)	ornamental extension to 'swash character' →
flowchart/flow diagram	diagram to show flow of process, activity or sequence of events; those used in data processing are of two types, systems flowcharts and program flowcharts:

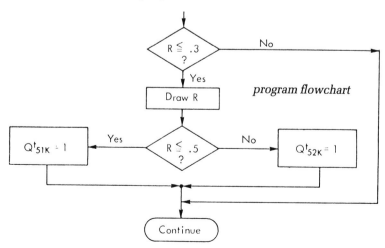

flowcharting symbols   those most commonly used in data processing are:

system flowcharting:

| process | manual operation | auxiliary operation | merge | extract | collate |

| sort | display | manual input | general input/output | connector | annotation |

| document | punched card | punched paper tape | magnetic tape | drum | disk |

additional symbols for program flowcharting:

| preparation | subroutine | decision | keying | terminal | off-page connector |

flower   see 'printer's flower'

flowline map   one in which route of traffic flow is shown by line and rate of flow by varying thickness of that line, thus:

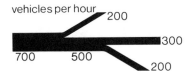

flush left/right   same as 'ranged left/right' →

flush mount   letterpress halftone plate with 'flange' → removed to fit up close to type matter or another plate

85

flyback
(computer graphics)

in 'CRT' → display, deflection of electronic beam back to beginning of new line, and back to beginning of whole frame:

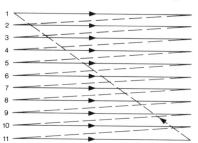

flyback interlacing
(computer graphics)

in 'CRT' → display, technique devised to reduce flicker:

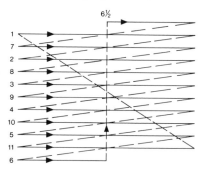

fly-fold

same as '4 page fold' (see 'folding methods')

fly leaf

that part of 'endpaper' → at front of book which is glued to first text leaf

flying paster

synonym for 'autopaster' →

FOB

initials of 'free on board', sometimes seen on invoices and implying free delivery of goods up to point of export

focal depth

see 'depth of focus'

focal length

notional measurement from camera lens to point at which distant image is in sharp focus, marked on lens by an 'f' followed by measurements from centre of lens to film when set at 'infinity', eg: 'f = 50mm':

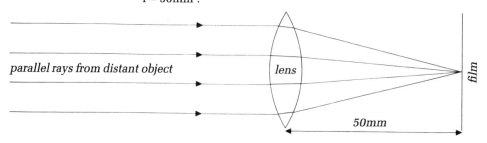

lenses are classified according to focal length and maximum 'aperture' →, and fall into general categories of short focus, standard and long focus:

image from whole negative through short focus lens

image from whole negative through long focus lens

foil   metallic mixture used in 'blocking' →; also, paper coated with metallic leaf or powder, used in boxmaking

fold-out   leaf of book extending beyond page width, so that it must be folded one or more times; also called 'throw-out' or 'pull-out':

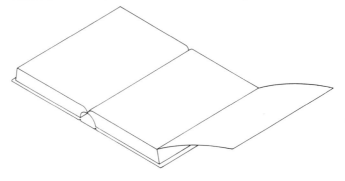

fold-to-paper	folding printed section (signature) by matching edges of sheet
fold-to-print	folding printed section (signature) matching print matter (usually page numbers); more accurate than 'fold-to-paper'
foldability (of paper)	capacity of particular paper to be folded without cracking
folder	piece of printed paper that is folded but not bound; also – confusingly – container for loose items of print
folding methods	standard patterns of paper folding in print are:

single fold   *double (gate) fold*   *double (concertina) fold*

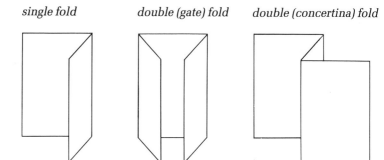

continuous fold (concertina)   *parallel fold*   *right angle fold*

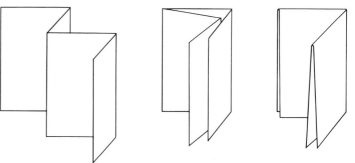

foliation (of book)	numbering leaves rather than pages, as distinct from 'pagination'
folio	cut or folded sheet that is half of basic sheet size; also used as synonym for 'page number'
follow copy	instruction to printer on manuscript or proof to set copy exactly as given, despite apparent errors
follow style	instruction to typesetter to adhere to previously specified style
folo	abbreviated spelling of 'follow', used in newspaper offices, as in instruction 'folo head', indicating that heading of feature is to be

repeated on subsequent page

font (US), **fount** (UK)	full set of characters of one size of type (hot metal) or range of sizes (photocomposition), comprising lower case, capitals, small caps (though not always), numerals, punctuation marks, reference marks, signs; US spelling is increasingly common in UK
foot	bottom of book →; also known as 'tail'
foot margin	see 'page'
footer (computers)	in VDU display, identifying element positioned at end of 'page' →
foredge, fore-edge	outside edge of book opposite back or spine (see also 'book')
foredge margin	see 'page'
foreground colours (VDU)	those available for colour characters in alphanumeric screen display
foreground processing (computers)	those operations that may be performed by user while machine continues other processing functions in background
forgiving system (computers)	one that allows beginners to commit errors without fearsome consequences; part of 'user-friendly' principle
form (US), **forme** (UK)	type matter, blocks and spacing material locked up in 'chase' → as complete letterpress printing unit; by extension, complete lithographic plate for printing one side of sheet
format	1) dimensions of trimmed sheet, page or book 2) general term for size, style and treatment of print matter 3) in photocomposition, coding arrangement whereby keyed-in text is converted to required typeface, size, line feed, measure, etc
format check (computers)	part of program that ensures item of data has correct character pattern
format effector (computers)	same as 'layout character' →
formatting	setting up command codes for computer-aided photocomposition, based on typographic mark-up
former	mechanism on some printing presses that makes fold in sheet
FORTRAN	see 'computer languages'
fortyeight sheet	poster size 120 × 480in (305 × 1220cm)
forwarding	in book production, originally those operations from completion of sewing to application of cover, now taken to include covering also

FOTS	initials of 'fibre optics' → *transmission system*
founder's/foundry type	type cast in very hard metal by typefounders for use in hand composition, as distinct from type cast in machine composition for one-job-only use
fount	see 'font'
fountain	on offset-litho machines, reservoir for supply of fountain solution (water, acid and gum) to dampening rollers; may also, confusingly, refer to 'ink duct' →, especially in US
4/4; 4/2; 4/1	in specification for print, shorthand for: 'four colours printing on both sides of sheet'; 'four colours one side, two colours on the other', and 'four colours one side, one colour on the other'
four-backing-one/ two/four	reference to printing imposition in which one side of sheet is printed in four colours, other side in one colour, two colours or four colours
four-colour process	full-colour printing from plates produced by photographic separation into subtractive primary colours (cyan, magenta, yellow) and black
Fourdrinier machine	one making continuous web (reel) of paper on moving belt of wire mesh
frame (computer graphics)	in VDU display, one screenful of data; 'page' → may be contained in one frame but not necessarily
frame buffer (computer graphics)	computer memory containing digital matrix that matches 'picture element' → pattern on screen
frame flyback (computer graphics)	see 'flyback'
frame-grabbing (computer graphics)	in VDU display, technique of holding and displaying, as long as desired, single frame on screen; may also relate to viewer-selected freeze-frame from moving television picture, especially in cable TV
frame mask	same as 'field area/size' →
free footage	in film animation, any shot that involves only camera or panning table movements with no need for additional drawn animation
free line-fall	same as 'ragged right' →; more common in US
free sheet (UK)	newspaper delivered free of charge; relies on advertising for financial support
freesheet (US)	paper that is free of mechanical wood pulp, using chemical pulp instead; known in UK as 'woodfree'
freeze-frame	in cinefilm and TV, special optical effect in which movement is

stopped at certain point in action; also called 'still-frame' in TV

french curves flat plastic shapes with combinations of curves, used for tracing:

french fold right-angle fold when used for invitations or similar items of print in order to have print on inside and outside with only one printing; see 'folding methods'

french sewing
(of book) method using only thread, with no cord or tape support

Fresnel lens in photography, special condenser lens used on spotlight to concentrate light beam or in viewing screen to assist focusing

frog eye synonym for 'hickie' →

front clipping plane
(computer graphics) same as 'hither plane' →

front end system
(computers) part of main computer, or separate computer, concerned with input

front lay edge see 'lay edges'

front matter (of book) same as 'prelims' → ; more common in US

front projection	in cinefilm, TV and still photography, taken to mean projection of background image via two-way mirror interposed between camera and main subject; from camera viewpoint, shadow cast by subject on screen is always hidden and projected image is not seen on subject if this is non-reflective:

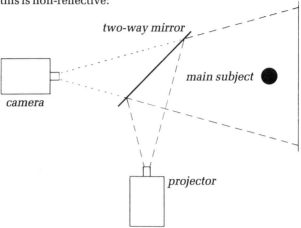

frontispiece, frontis	illustration on preliminary page of book, usually facing title page
frustrum	that part of cone or pyramid remaining when top part has been cut off parallel to base:

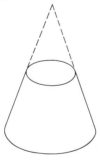

FTS	initials of *f*acsimile *t*ransmission *s*ystem
fudge	stop-press matter in newspaper contained within 'fudge-box' on printing press
fugitive colour	coloured ink that fades on exposure to certain light or humidity conditions
fugitive ink	one which fades or changes colour on exposure to light, as distinct from 'light-fast' or 'permanent' ink
full bound	in book binding, case that is fully covered with single piece of material, as distinct from 'half bound' → and 'quarter bound' →
full colour	subject treated in 'four colour process' →

full-faced type	US synonym for 'titling' →
full-out	instruction to printer to set line or lines of type without indentation
full point	printer's term for 'full stop' or 'period'
full-sized fraction	one made up from full-sized numerals, thus: 1/3
function character (computers)	same as 'control character' →
function codes	in photocomposition, those codes regulating setting down of characters, as distinct from codes that generate characters themselves
function key (computers)	one on console keyboard that activates 'control character' →
functional character	same as 'control character' →
furnish	mixture of materials used in making of paper
furniture	in letterpress, material used to take up space around type and blocks before locking up forme for printing

G

galley	metal tray used to hold composed type before it is made up in page; also used to mean 'galley proof' (see below)
galley proof	rough proof, in long strip, of composed type before it is made up in page; sometimes called 'slip proof'
galley slave	slang term for 'compositor' (archaic, but too good to leave out)
gang-ups	several print jobs run off on same sheet of paper, which is then cut up into individual pieces
garalde	British Standards' term for those typefaces otherwise known as 'old faces' → ; see also 'typeface classification'
garland	sometimes used to describe book of poems or prose extracts
gas plasma display	same as 'plasma panel display' →
gate	switch in any electronic circuit
gate-fold	see 'folding methods'
GATF	initials of *G*raphic *A*rts *T*echnical *F*oundation, based in Pittsburgh, Pa.

gathering	arranging sheets or sections in correct order so as to make up book:

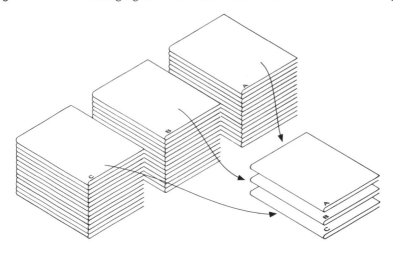

sections (signatures) gathered in reverse order according to signature marks at foot of first page of each section

GDT (computers)	initials of '*g*raphic *d*isplay *t*erminal' →
gel	abbreviation for 'gelatine filter'; placed over photographic light source to alter colour balance
generic codes	in word-processing and photocomposition, those codes appended to input text that control style and specification
geometric figures	see 'angles', 'quadrilaterals', 'regular polygons' and 'regular solids'
geometric sans-serif	one constructed of geometric shapes, with even line thickness and usually having single storey 'a' and 'g':

ABCDEFGHIJ abcdefghij

gestalt	German for 'configuration'; Gestalt School of Psychology relates to ways in which images are perceived and understood
ghosting	1) weak impression resulting from inability of machine to cope with heavy inking 2) shadow effect of image on television screen, caused by interference with broadcast signal
gigo, GIGO (computers)	initials of '*g*arbage *i*n – *g*arbage *o*ut', name given to principle which holds that no computer program can produce good output from bad input
glassine	transparent, glazed paper used for wrappings and window envelopes

glitch, glytch (computers)	fault in machine or process, particularly electronic
global search-and-replace	in photocomposition, facility that permits machine to locate character, word or phrase wherever it occurs in document and correct it on basis of single command
gloss ink	printing ink having high proportion of varnish, to give shiny effect
glossary function	in word-processing, insertion into new text of pre-set word or phrase by operator, using special command code
glossy	said of paper (whether photographic or printing) having highly polished surface
glyphic (of typeface)	one that has origin in chiselled, rather than calligraphic, model:

abcdefghijklm
ABCDEFGHIJ

g/m²	abbreviation for 'grammes per square metre'; method of denoting substance of paper by weight, now standard in most of Europe including UK; this weight factor is known as 'grammage'
GMT (computers)	initials of *graphic mouse technology* (see 'mouse')
golden section	harmonious proportion arising from division of any line A–C at point B so that AB is to AC as BC is to AB; this ratio (1:1.618) provides dimensions of 'golden rectangle':

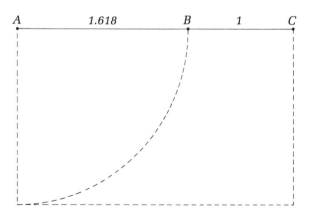

goldenrod	opaque, pre-ruled paper used for litho 'flat' →
golf-ball	colloquial name for spherical typing head of IBM 72 typewriter and its derivatives

gothic	same as 'black letter' →, but in US refers to sans-serif typefaces, particularly of 19th-century vintage; best avoided except as part of name of typeface
gouache	opaque, gum-based paint soluble in water; particularly suitable for use in presentation visuals and artwork for reproduction
GPO	1) initials of (US) *G*overnment *P*rinting *O*ffice 2) initials of (UK) *G*eneral *P*ost *O*ffice, now called Post Office
grain (of film)	in photography, clumps of minute silver grains which form image in film emulsion; may become visible as speckle pattern due to excessive enlargement
grain (of paper)	see 'machine direction'
grain direction (of paper)	dominant direction of cellulose fibres, following direction of paper-making machine; paper is stronger under tension in machine direction and is less liable to shrink or stretch
-gram	suffix denoting 'thing written or drawn' (see also '-graph')
grammage	see 'g/m²'
grammes	see 'g/m²'
graph	see 'coordinate graph', 'bar graph', 'logarithmic graph', 'pie graph', 'scatter graph' and 'star graph'; for another meaning, see 'graph theory' below
-graph	suffix denoting either 'thing written or drawn' or 'thing for recording'
graph plotter (computers)	output device that draws image on paper or film under instruction from computer; there are two main types, 'drum plotter' and 'flat-bed plotter':

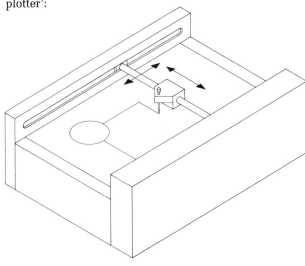

graph theory	one dealing with geometric figures (graphs), consisting of points (vertices) and lines (edges), used to express relations and connexions; see also 'network diagram'
graphic (of typeface)	one which suggests origin in drawn, rather than written, model:

ABCDEF
claim as valid

graphic arts camera	see 'process camera'
graphic arts quality	said of computer-generated text printout that is of quality comparable to that of conventional typesetting
graphic/graphical display terminal	electronic device used in computer-aided photocomposition and other graphic visualizing tasks
graphic tablet (computers)	interactive input device consisting of electronically sensitive, gridded board displaying graphic/alphanumeric options, activated by touch of electronic pen to compose images on VDU screen; also called 'markup board':

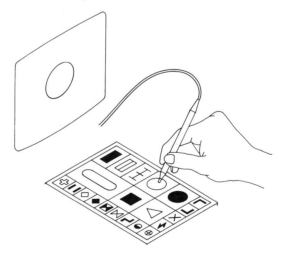

graphics characters	in photocomposition, those added to alphanumeric set to provide graphic 'building blocks'
graphics standards (computers)	those agreed as part of interfacing arrangements between systems
graphics subroutine package (computer graphics)	one enabling users of computer graphics systems to assemble their own software

97

graticule	cross-line grid laid over image so as to provide key to features within it (eg: lines of longitude and latitude on maps)
graunch (computers)	some unplanned error in machine function
grave accent	see 'accented (diacritical) signs'
gravure	same as 'photogravure' →
gray literature	printed matter, such as reports, not formally published, listed or priced
gray (grey) scale	one used in photomechanical reproduction to check correct exposure and development time
grayware (computers)	human involvement in computer processing from gray (grey) matter of brain
greaseproof	translucent paper specially treated for use as food wrapping
Greek alphabet	characters in Greek alphabet are:

Αα	*alpha*	Ηη	*eta*	Νν	*nu*	Ττ	*tau*
Ββ	*beta*	Θθ	*theta*	Ξξ	*xi/si*	Υυ	*upsilon*
Γγ	*gamma*	Ιι	*iota*	Οο	*omicron*	Φφ	*phi*
Δδ	*delta*	Κκ	*kappa*	Ππ	*pi*	Χχ	*chi*
Εε	*epsilon*	Λλ	*lambda*	Ρϱ	*rho*	Ψψ	*psi*
Ζζ	*zeta*	Μμ	*mu*	Σσς	*sigma*	Ωω	*omega*

grid	see 'layout grid'
grid constraint (computer graphics)	feature that automatically moves screen 'cursor' → to nearest grid intersection whenever point is manually entered
grid (matrix)	in photocomposition, an 'image-carrier' → in grid form
gripper edge	edge of sheet that is held by mechanical gripper when being fed into printing press, that is, leading or front edge; sometimes called 'front lay edge'
gripper margin	that margin that has to be allowed for on sheet so that it can be gripped without affecting area of job when trimmed
grotesque	kind of sans-serif typeface dating from mid-19th century (also known as 'gothic' in US), as distinguished from 'humanist sans-serif' → and 'geometric sans-serif' →:

abcdefghijk
ABCDEFG

groundwood pulp	synonym for 'mechanical pulp' → ; term more commonly used in US
gsm	earlier, now incorrect, form of 'g/m²' → though still in use
guard book	any book bound with guards (see 'guarding') but particularly one containing different paper stock or samples
guarding	method of attaching single leaf to section of book or periodical, as more secure alternative to 'tipping in/on' →:

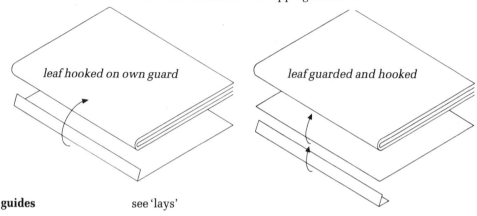

leaf hooked on own guard *leaf guarded and hooked*

guides	see 'lays'
guillemets	French quotation marks « thus »; also used in some German texts
guillotine	machine for trimming paper or board consisting of strong clamp and knife blade moving up and down within vertical groove; may be controlled by computer program
gutter	space between pages, including allowance for trim, when imposed in formes (see 'imposition'); sometimes wrongly used to describe channel between two columns of type

H

H & J, H/J, h & j	initials of 'hyphenation and justification'; see 'end-of-line decisions'
háček	see 'accented (diacritical) signs'
hache	symbol denoting 'number' in US and 'space' in UK:
hachures	in some maps, lines drawn down slopes in direction of steepest gradients, placed closer together where slope is steeper
hairline	finest printable line, as used for serifs in 'modern-face' →
hairspace	in traditional hand composition, thinnest available space; used mainly for letter spacing

halation	in photography, halo effect produced by bright light source contrasting with darker surround or silhouette:

half bound	book having case of which spine and corners are covered in one material (eg: cloth), and rest with another (eg: paper):

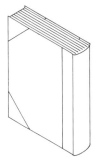

half-sheet work	form of imposition in which section is made from one half of whole sheet so that two identical sections are made from each half (see also 'work-and-turn' and 'work-and-tumble')
half-title	right-hand page preceding title page of book, containing title only
half up	artwork prepared one-and-a-half times reproduced size, so as to ensure fine detail and accuracy
halftone	continous tone subject, whether original or converted for reproduction, in contrast to line subject
halftone process	photomechanical reproduction of continuous-tone originals by means of technique that converts image into minute graded dots giving appearance of continuous tone, achieved by photographing original through glass or film screen containing pattern of fine

100

crossed lines which split image into white or black dots according to variation of dark and light tones in original:

standard ruling for halftone screens are:

rulings per inch	50	65	85	100	120	133	150	175	200
rulings per centimetre	20	26	30	40	48	54	60	70	80

hand cursor
(computers)
input device used in conjunction with 'digitizing pad' → , having cross-hairs for exact location of coordinates

handshaking
(computers)
operation that coordinates and harmonizes communication between components in system

hand-sorted punched card
same as 'edge-notched card' →

hanging indent
in typesetting, indenting all lines in paragraph except first one; also known as 'reverse indent'

hanging punctuation
punctuation marks set outside type measure as stylistic refinement

hard-backed book
one with stiff board cover

hard copy
(computers)
1) computer output on paper, often to provide permanent record of information displayed on VDU
2) typed duplicate produced by computer-driven photocomposing system, to check accuracy of input before setting

hard-copy keyboard
one that produces text on paper as on traditional typewriter, in contrast to 'soft-copy keyboard' →

hard disk (computers)	type of 'magnetic disk' →
hard dot	halftone image with dot strength that cannot be increased or decreased except minimally
hard grade paper	in photography, one giving high contrast image
hard sized paper	material containing large amount of 'size' → ; usually said of 'writing' →
hardware (computers)	physical components of computer system, as against 'software' →
hardwired (computers)	said of any device that is pre-programmed and whose program cannot be changed
Hart's Rules	publication setting out rules for compositors and printer readers in connexion with spelling, hyphenation, abbreviation, punctuation, etc
head	top edge of book →
head (electronics)	electromagnet designed to 'read', record or erase signals on magnetic tape, disk or drum
head- and tail bands	in 'cased/case-bound book' → , folded strips of cloth added at top and bottom of spine to cover up back edges of sections
head bolt	thickening of sheet at last (head) fold before trimming:

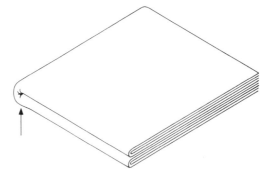

headliner	same as 'photoheadliner' and 'photodisplay unit'
heat sealing	closing plastic bag or wrapper by partially melting edge under heat
heat-set inks	those designed for quick-drying by application of heat, which vaporizes oil content and allows residue to harden more speedily
heavy (type)	sometimes used instead of 'bold' → to denote typeface variant
hectography	process of printing limited number of copies by means of gelatin plate and special ink

height-to-paper	same as 'type-height' →
heliogravure	form of 'photoengraving' →
helix	'locus' → of point that moves round circumference of cylinder or cone and axially at same time, with ratio of two movements constant, as in corkscrew:

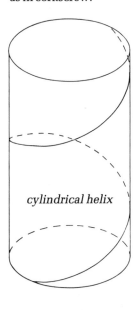
cylindrical helix

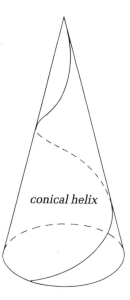
conical helix

heuristics	study of problem-solving by means of trial and error, involving successive evaluations at each step towards final solution; as distinct from 'algorithmics' →
hex pad (computers)	slang for 'hexadecimal' → keyboard, often used as input device for 'microprocessors' →
hexadecimal code	one with base, or 'radix' →, of 16 instead of 10 (decimal) or 2 (binary); usual hexadecimal notation is 0 1 2 3 4 5 6 7 8 9 A B C D E F 10
hexagon	six-sided figure (see 'regular polygon')
hexagram	figure formed by two intersecting equilateral triangles:

hickie, hickey	in printing, speck of dust, bit of loose ink or other intrusive matter which has become stuck to type matter plate or offset blanket and shows up as haloed spot

| **hidden-edge/line removal** (computers) | function available in many graphic display programs by which edges of 'wire-frame pictures' → not visible from chosen viewpoint are edited out of display: |

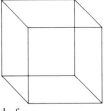 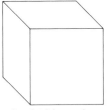

before · *after hidden-edge removal*

hieratic script later, abridged form of hieroglyphic writing

hieroglyph Greek for 'holy carving'; used especially to describe ancient Egyptian inscriptions and writings; basically pictogrammatic, though 'ideograms' → and 'phonograms' → were also used

high gloss ink one having 'vehicle' → so composed that ink does not penetrate deeply into paper and so has varnished appearance

high key photographic image in which, by lighting and/or processing, most of tones are very light:

high level language (computers) programming language composed of words and symbols that are already familiar to ordinary user, rather than one oriented to computer's machine code

high resolution scanning electron-beam 'raster scan' → producing 'pixel array' → of 2048 × 2048

highlight halftone same as 'drop-out halftone' →

histogram 'coordinate graph' → in which frequency percentage is plotted as 'ordinate' → and varying quantity as 'abscissa' → usually as 'bar graph' →

hit-on-the-fly printer
(computers)

printout device in which type head does not pause during impression, thus saving stop-and-start time

hither plane
(computer graphics)

one forming front plane of finite 'view volume' → in 3D perspective; also known as 'front clipping plane'

HLS colour model
(computer graphics)

one promoted by Tektronix Inc, based on 'Ostwald colour system' →; H = hue, L = lightness, S = saturation:

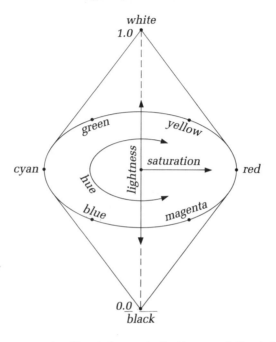

holdout

property of 'coated paper' – that keeps printing ink from being absorbed

holding line

US term for 'keyline' →

holo-

prefix meaning 'whole'

hologram/holograph image

one that gives three-dimensional illusion without use of camera: laser beam (known as 'coherent light') is split so that diffraction patterns are produced on photographic film; these reconstitute image of subject when illuminated by light from similar laser

holograph

manuscript wholly written in author's own hand

hooking

see 'guarding'

horizontal format

same as 'landscape format' →, more commonly used in US

horizontal raster count
(computer graphics)

number of horizontal divisions in 'raster' →

host computer	large machine servicing guest terminals that are connected either by fixed links or 'dialup' → lines
hot melt	adhesive used in book binding which needs heating before application
hot metal composition	any typeset matter originating in hot metal casting: Monotype, Linotype, Intertype and Ludlow
hot press lettering	depositing metal foil image from type, by means of heat and pressure, onto board; used for shop display cards, TV captions, etc.
house corrections	proof corrections of printer's errors, made by printer's reader and shown on 'master proof' →; rectified at printer's expense
house style	imposed rules of design by which commercial, professional, charitable or state-supported body establishes consistency, coherence and recognizability in its publicity, promotion, stationery, packaging and distribution; also known as 'corporate identity'; may also refer to sets of rules for printers, as 'Hart's Rules' →
housekeeping (computers)	those routines not directly concerned with problem-solving but with routine maintenance
HSV colour model (computer graphics)	one proposed by A S Smith in 1978 for electronic colour transmission, derived in part from 'Ostwald colour system' →; H = hue, S = saturation, V = value:

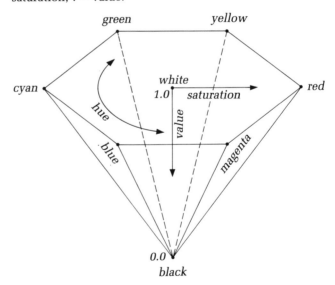

h/t	abbreviation for 'halftone' →
hue	means of distinguishing one colour from another by measuring predominating wavelengths of coloured substances; see also 'Munsell colour system'

humanist	applied to typefaces generally, distinguishes those roman and venetian designs based on revived carolingian scripts used by Italian Renaissance scholars in 15th century
humanist sans-serif	one based on proportions of roman and venetian typefaces, usually having two-storey 'a' and 'g':

TASTES change

Hunter Lab values	US system for measuring colour
hyperbola	'locus' → of point that moves so that ratio of its distances from fixed point and from fixed straight line is constant and greater than one; see also 'conic sections'
hyperfocal distance	in photography, distance from camera lens to nearest object which is acceptably sharp when focused on infinity
hyphenation	splitting one word or compounding two or more words by use of hyphen; used rather inaccurately to describe word-breaking at end of line of type
hyphenless justification	phototypesetting mode that avoids word-breaks at end of lines, inevitably at cost of wider word spacing or character spacing
hypo	slang for sodium hyposulphate, wrongly supposed to be fixing solution for photographic film and paper (it is, in fact, sodium thiosulphate)

I

ibc	initials of 'inside back cover'
ibid	abbreviation for *ibidem*, Latin for 'in the same place'; used in footnotes to refer to book, chapter or passage already referred to
IBM pica	confusing modification of traditional 'pica' → made by multinational company, whereby *their* pica is defined as exactly one-sixth of an inch, or 0.1666 . . . in, instead of 0.166604 in
ICOGRADA	initials of *International Council of Graphic Design Associations*, founded 1963 to act as talking shop for professional, educational and technical aspects of graphic design
icon, ikon	Greek for 'image, likeness', traditionally applied to representation of sacred figure, then adopted by 'semiotics' → theorists to mean 'sign

having some resemblance or analogy to that which it refers to'; now also used by users and makers of computer 'peripherals' → to denote display symbol (eg: on keyboard) representing function or device, as an alternative to verbal description

ICR — initials of *i*ntegrated *c*olour *r*emoval: same as 'achromatic colour correction' →

ID (pron: eye-dee) — 1) abbreviation for 'corporate *id*entity' →
2) abbreviation for '*id*entification', used during 'log-on' →

ideal format — in photography, increasingly popular negative size of 60 × 70mm, devised to satisfy those wanting rectangular format larger than, and not so elongated as, 35mm format (24 × 36mm):

idem — Latin for '(by) the same'; used in footnotes

ideogram/graph — character that symbolizes an idea by representing associated object but does not express sounds of its name; many Chinese characters are ideograms

idiot tape — see 'unjustified tape'

ie — initials of *id est*, Latin for 'that is'

ifc — initials of '*i*nside *f*ront *c*over'

IFD — initials of *I*nternational *F*ederation for *D*ocumentation, also known as 'FID' from French word order

IFIP — initials of *I*nternational *F*ederation for *I*nformation *P*rocessing

IIP — initials of '*I*nstitute of *I*ncorporated *P*hotographers'; body representing those practising professionally as photographers in UK

Ikarus (computer graphics) — name of computer program developed by Peter Karow of Hamburg, Germany to permit design of new weights and other modifications of existing typeface designs

image area — inkable and printable area of printing plate

image capture/ grabbing (computer graphics) — technique of absorbing 3D or 2D images into computer store, usually by means of video camera

image carrier	useful term covering those components of photocomposition systems (either disk, grid, drum or film strip) having same function as set of type matrices in machine composition; also called 'image master'
image data tablet (computers)	same as 'digitizing pad' →
image master	synonym for 'image carrier' →
imitation art	cheaper substitute for art paper, in which clay content is added during paper-making instead of being laid on subsequently
impact printing	any conventional printing process, such as letterpress, lithography or gravure, as against 'non-impact printing' →
impose	to arrange type and other print matter in pages and lock up as 'forme' → for printing
imposed proof	proof taken from forme; also called 'sheet proof'
imposition	arrangement of pages for printing on sheet, in unit called 'forme' → so that they will be in correct sequence when folded to form section (signature); simplest imposition is for 4 pages:

 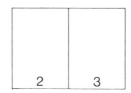

and 16 page imposition is typical:

5	12	6	8		7	10	11	9
4	13	16	1		2	15	14	3

other common impositions are for 8 pages and 32 pages, though 12, 24 and 36 pages are also feasible; imposition plans are vital planning tools since they show instantly which pages are on same side of sheet, how to arrange colour economically and how to re-arrange imposition if particular colour sequence is required (see also 'half-sheet work', 'work and tumble', 'work and turn' and 'work and twist')

impossible triangle	representation of object that cannot exist in reality, devised by psychologists LS and R Penrose in 1958:

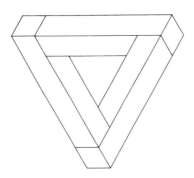

impression	any printed copy made from type matter or plates, and physical action that produces it; also, by extension, whole print run (used in connexion with number of copies printed)
impression cylinder	that part of 'cylinder press' → which receives paper, takes it into contact with inked type matter or plate and makes impression
imprint (printer's)	printer's name, usually shown inconspicuously on reverse of title page or at foot of last page
imprint (publisher's)	publisher's name printed on title page of book
imprint page	reverse of title page of book, used for information about copyright conditions, printing history and printer; also called 'biblio' page
in-betweens	in film animation, those drawings (often made by another hand) which fill in movement between 'extremes' →
in-camera process	one in which development of image takes place within camera, as in Polaroid cameras
in-house/in-plant print	work executed by organization whose main business is not printing but which has its own printing plant
in-house software (computers)	'software' → devised by computer users for their own special use, as contrasted to software package bought in
in pro	abbreviation of 'in proportion', used when giving instructions to reduce or enlarge originals in proportion to one another
increment	in general, an increase or measure of increase; see 'line increment'
incunabulum (pl: incunabula)	Latin for 'from the cradle'; used to describe an early book, especially one printed before 1501
indent	to leave blank space at beginning of line of type, usually first line of paragraph (see also 'hanging indent')

index	alphabetical list of subjects dealt with in book, with relevant page numbers; but see also 'step', 'tab' and 'thumb' index
index board	materials with high machine finish, produced in range of tints for use in card index systems
india paper	very thin paper used for books where lightness and compactness are called for
indirect letterpress	same as 'letterset' →
inferior figure/letter	small character set to appear below level of normal characters of typeface; eg: H_2SO_4
infinite scrolling (computers)	capacity of computer program to 'scroll' → through document of any length in continuous operation instead of having to deal with it page by page
informatics	jargon for study of information technology
information theory	extension of 'communication theory' → from mathematics into other, less specific fields of science:

model of information process on which information theory is based

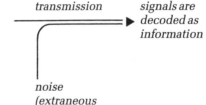

source of information selected for transmission ▶ information is coded as signals ── transmission ═▶ signals are decoded as information ▶ destination of this information

noise (extraneous signals)

infra-red	near visible waves in 'electromagnetic spectrum' → which can show on some photographic materials
injection-moulding	injecting liquefied plastics material into space between matched moulds, thus:

material injected here

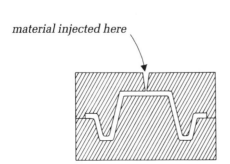
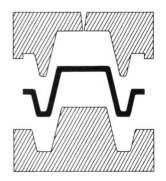

ink duct	ink reservoir on printing machine from which supply of ink is regulated; sometimes referred to (especially in US) as 'ink fountain'; see also 'split duct/fountain' and 'fountain'
ink duplicating	simple planographic printing process for up to 1,000 copies, using negative stencil master produced by drawing or typing; also known as 'mimeography', from trade name 'Mimeograph'
ink-jet plotter (computers)	output device that sprays image, often multi-coloured, onto paper by means of very fine jet
ink-jet printer	computer output device using high speed ink jets projected onto paper to make desired image, usually of alphanumeric characters:

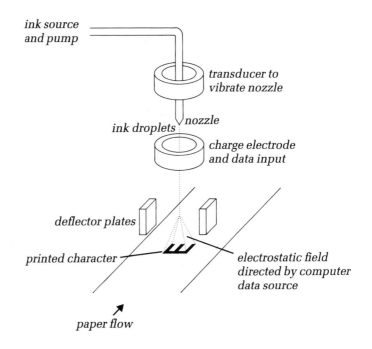

ink squash	printing characteristic, particularly of letterpress, in which ink spreads beyond outline of impression surface
inking roller	that part of printing machine used to transfer ink from ink supply to printing surface
inline (type)	typeface in which fine white line runs through centre of strokes:

inner form/forme	form/forme → that contains innermost spread of folded section

112

input	expression used in computer-controlled operations to describe any information (data) to be processed
inserting	adding separately printed piece into book or periodical after binding
insetting	placing one unit of book or periodical into another, 'insetted work' is so called to distinguish it from gathered work (see 'gathering'):

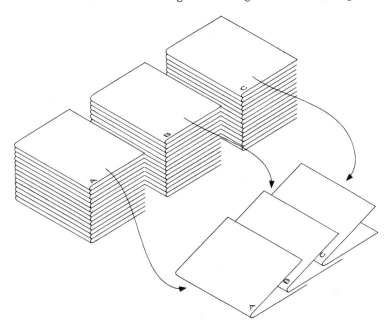

inside margin	same as 'back margin' (see 'page') but not recommended because less clearly linked with 'back' of book
intaglio	general description for those printing processes (eg: photogravure) in which inked image is in etched or engraved recesses below surface of printing plate
integer	any whole number, as against fraction
integrated circuit (electronics)	one in which all components exist as chemical constructions within a single, minute sliver, almost invariably of silicon, a semi-conductor (material whose conductivity increases at high temperatures and decreases at low temperatures)
interactive display (computers)	one that permits user to input data or instructions in response to displayed information
interactive mode (computers)	operating method in which user converses directly with computer and obtains immediate reply; also known as 'conversational mode' (though that implies an even more intimate connexion)

interface	useful jargon for place where interaction occurs between two systems or processes, or between human and machine
interlacing (computer graphics)	see 'flyback interlacing'
interlay	prepared paper inserted between letterpress printing plate and its mount to build up strength of tone in darker areas and decrease it in lighter areas
interleaving	to place unprinted sheets between printed sheets as they come off press, to prevent 'set-off' →; known as 'slip-sheeting' in US
interlinear spacing	in photocomposition, equivalent of 'leading'
international paper sizes	see 'A, B and C Series'
international phonetic alphabet	1) agreed code for spelling out letters of words over telephone:

A	Alfa	J	Julia	S	Sierra
B	Bravo	K	Kilo	T	Tango
C	Charlie	L	Lima	U	Uniform
D	Delta	M	Mike	V	Victor
E	Echo	N	November	W	Whisky
F	Foxtrot	O	Oscar	X	X-ray
G	Golf	P	Papa	Y	Yankee
H	Hotel	Q	Quebec	Z	Zulu
I	India	R	Romeo		

2) special type characters (not properly an alphabet) designed to represent accurately all speech sounds, eg:

'ɪŋglɪʃ prənʌnsɪ 'eɪʃn

internegative, interneg	intermediate stage between positive original (opaque or transparent) and print
interpolation (computer graphics)	adding intermediate values in computer graphics display between existing values, especially in variable tone and colour shaded subject matter
interrogating typewriter (computers)	'teleprinter' → used for direct transmission of data from computer to distant terminal and vice-versa
Intertype	obsolescent type composing machine that produces a line of type (slug) in one piece, similar to Linotype
Intrafax	name of closed circuit 'facsimile transmission' → system developed by Western Union

inverted commas	pair of commas inverted thus " to signify opening of quotation; also known as 'turned commas'
involute	'locus' → of point fixed on line that rolls, without slipping, around polygon:

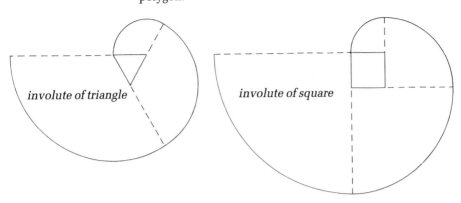

involute of triangle

involute of square

I/O (computers)	initials of 'input/output'
Ionic	range of typefaces dating from mid-19th century, slab-seriffed with slight bracketing, much used in newspaper work:

abcdefghijklmnopqrstuvwxz
ABCDEFGHIJKLMNOPQRS

iph	initials of 'impressions per hour'; measure of rate of printing machine
IR	initials of information retrieval
iris (of camera)	usual form of diaphragm that controls 'aperture' →
isarithm	same as 'isoline' →
ISBD	initials of International Standard Bibliographical Description: agreed convention for description of documents, introduced by American Library Association
ISBN	initials of 'International Standard Book Number', ten-digit number allocated to each published book, with separate number for each edition; first part of number is group identifier (ie: country or group of countries), second part is publisher identifier, third part is title identifier and last part is single check digit
iso-	prefix meaning 'same' (as in 'isometric')
ISO	initials of 'International Standards Organization', body based in Switzerland who publish many Standards and Recommendations, including 'A, B and C Series' of paper and envelope sizes →, 'film speed' ratings → and an ever-increasing number relating to publishing (see Bibliography)

115

isoline	line on map drawn through locations having same value of particular feature, eg: rainfall; isobar connects locations with same value of air pressure, isotherm with same value of temperature:

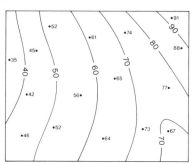

isometric projection	'axonometric projection' → in which axes are arranged at 120° to each other and all dimensions along axes are in same scale ratio
isopleth	same as 'isoline' →
Isotype	acronym for '*I*nternational *S*ystem *o*f *T*ypographical *P*icture *E*ducation, system of pictorial graph-making pioneered by Otto Neurath in Vienna from 1924
IT	initials of '*i*nformation *t*echnology'
italic	originally, typeface of cursive character based on chancery italic (ie: Italian) handwriting; now used for any face with characters which incline noticeably to right, though some of these are more properly called 'sloped roman':

specialized   *documents*

true italic   sloped roman

ITD	initials of *i*nteractive *t*ypographic *d*isplay
ivory board	high-grade white board of even finish with clear, translucent look-through, used mainly for business and greeting cards

J

jacket	same as 'book jacket' →
jaggies (computer graphics)	irregular effect apparent in VDU graphics display, in which curves and diagonals are imperfectly rendered by rectilinear scanning

pattern; also known as 'aliasing'

jet printing
(computer graphics)   see 'ink-jet printing'

jim-dash   short rule between newspaper items

jitter   image irregularity in output of 'facsimile transmission' → system

jobbing printer   one who takes on various sorts of work and is not tied to one
                             particular kind (called 'job shop' in US)

jogging (printing)   aligning edges of stack of paper sheets by using vibration

joystick (computers)   input device used to control movement of images on VDU, handy for
                             computer games; also known as 'paddle':

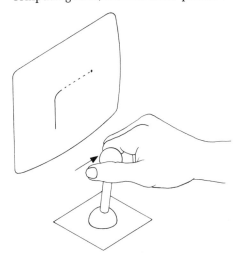

joyswitch   variant of 'joystick' → that moves only at constant rate in any chosen
(computers)   direction

judder   distortion of transmitted image during 'facsimile transmission' →
                             caused by vibration in machine

jump   carry over portion of newspaper or periodical feature from one page
                             to another, hence 'jump-line'

jump-cut   in cinefilm and TV, any cut between two takes which jars on one's
                             eyes; may be intentional or just bad camerawork and editing

justification range   definition of maximum and minimum permitted word spaces in
                             typesetting where both left-and right-hand edges are to be
                             'justified' →

justified (of type)   lines of type set so as to fill 'measure' →; less accurately, but usefully,
                             lines of type that range visually on both sides

K

k	abbreviation for 'kilo-' →; sometimes, most improperly, used to mean 'kilobyte' →, for which correct abbreviation is 'kb'
K	sometimes used in 'four colour process' → specification and correction to denote 'key', ie: key colour, usually black; also, improperly, used as abbreviation for 'kilo-' (should be lower case)
kanji	name for selection of Chinese ideogram characters (about 5,000) used to write Japanese language; smaller selection of 1,850 of these were chosen by Japanese government for use in newspapers and official publications:
kb (computers)	abbreviation for 'kilobyte' →
keep down	instruction to compositor: keep type in lower-case (newspaper term)
keep in	instruction to compositor: use narrow word spaces
keep out	instruction to compositor: use wide word spaces (same as 'drive out')
keep standing	instruction to printer to keep type matter ready for possible reprinting
keep up	instruction to printer: keep type in caps (newspaper term)
kern	part of piece of type sticking out to one side of body so that it overlaps onto adjacent piece:

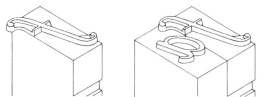

kerning	applied to type which kerns, now used in photocomposition to describe a backspacing technique whereby one character may be tucked into another, thus: Ta, WA; also applied to dubious practice of compressing copy to fit line by 'minus' or abnormally close letter-spacing
kerning pairs	in photocomposition, nominated pairs of characters such as AT, AV, AW, LT, TA, Ta, Te, To, Tu, Va, Ve, Vo, Vu, Wa, We, Wo, Wu, that are close-fitted so as to offset irregular letterspacing effect caused by their conjunction
kettle stitch	type of stitch used to secure one 'section' → to another

118

key-driven (computers)	said of computer requiring operator to use keyboard in order to instruct and communicate with it
key plate	in colour printing, that plate which is to print first, providing key for registering subsequent colours (also called 'first colour down')
keyboarding	in machine- and photocomposition, first operation of typing in copy to be set; until advent of photocomposition, operator was known as 'compositor' (US: 'typographer'), but is now increasingly described as 'keyboard operator' or even 'keyboardist', especially when producing 'unjustified tape' →
keyline	outline drawn on artwork to indicate area of solid or position of halftone image; also called 'holding line'
keys	in film animation, same as 'extremes' →
keystone distortion (computer graphics)	typical distortion of CRT image:

keystroke	one action on keyboard, used as measure of input to text-handling system for calculating cost and/or time taken
keyword index, **keyword-from-title** **index** (computers)	one using significant word or words in title of written work by which it may be identified for retrieval, especially from computer-operated memory store; keywords may be shown in context of rest of title (KWIC) or outside it (KWOC) →
kicker	line of type above or below title of newspaper or periodical feature
kill	delete unwanted copy or 'distribute' → unwanted type matter
kill the widow!	colourful way of instructing sub-editor or operator of typesetting machine to remove an undesired single word (widow) which forms last line of paragraph
kilo-	prefix meaning one thousand as in kilometre; but see 'kilobyte' below
kilobyte (computers)	literally means one thousand 'bytes' →, but actually stands for 1024 bytes, a 'binary thousand' or 2^{10}
kinematic program (computer graphics)	one that is devised to simulate action of design with moving parts
kiss impression	in letterpress, ideal impression whereby image is rich and well inked but paper shows no sign of embossing effect

kph *keystrokes per hour*: measure of keyboarding speed

KWIC/KWOC initials of '*keyword-in-c*ontext index' and '*keyw*ord-*o*ut-of-*c*ontext'
indexes (computers) (see 'keyword index')

L

L ruling machine one that draws rulings in two directions in one pass of machine

label (computers) heading allocated to particular procedural step in entering program routine or subroutine

lacquer colourless varnish giving high gloss finish; may be applied to covers as alternative to 'lamination' →

lacuna missing portion of text resulting from damage to manuscript or book

laid paper uncoated paper that shows faint pattern of ribbed lines – 'laid' lines and 'chain' lines – when looked at through light and slight corrugations on one side (known as 'wire-side'), caused during making

Lambert's projections see 'cylindrical projections' and 'zenithal projections'

lamination application of transparent plastic film to sheet of paper or board, giving hard, glossy surface

LAN abbreviation for '*l*ocal *a*rea *n*etwork' →

landscape format describes proportion of film, photoprint, artwork or any piece of print matter in which height is appreciably shorter than width

lap small overlap allowed when two printed colours abut, so as to prevent risk of any gap resulting from slight lack of register

lap-dissolve technique involving use of two slide projectors and linking unit to dissolve succeeding projected images from one into the other:

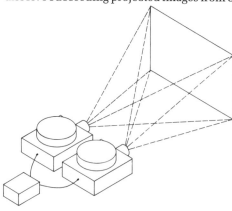

lap-top computer	one having 'flat panel display' → and of small size suitable for easy transport; may be battery operated
large face	larger of two sizes available on same body of typeface
laser	acronym for *l*ight *a*mplification by *s*timulated *e*mission of *r*adiation; essentially, high energy light beam device with wide application in communications industry:
laser printer (computer graphics)	use of 'laser' → as image-creating component in 'non-impact printer' →
Lasercomp	trade name for photocomposition system involving use of laser beam
latent image	in photography, any image capable of being developed chemically
lateral shift (camera)	movement on most technical cameras and some small format cameras whereby lens panel is moved sideways in relation to camera back
Latin (of typefaces)	in general, all typefaces derived from western European letterforms, as distinct from, say, Arabic or Hebrew; more specifically (and confusingly), those typefaces having 'wedge-serifs' →
lay edges	those edges of sheet that are presented to side 'lays' of printing machine; front edge is usually called 'gripper edge' → though 'front lay edge' is equally correct
layout	plan designed to show how printed result is to be obtained and give some idea of how it would look
layout character	one employed, usually via keyboard, to control layout of printout or typeset matter
layout grid	pre-printed sheet with lines showing basic pattern to be followed in designing layouts or preparing paste-up artwork:

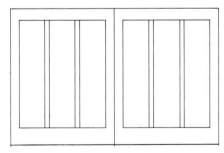

lays	on printing machines, devices at front and side to which paper is fed before processing (printing, folding, stamping, perforating, etc); more commonly known in US as 'guides'
LC	initials of *L*ibrary of *C*ongress

LCD	initials of '*l*iquid *c*rystal *d*isplay': type of electronic display for editing terminals, pocket calculators and the like, in form of black or silver characters on coloured or near-white ground
LDX	initials of *l*ong *d*istance *x*erox: method combining 'xerography' → with 'facsimile transmission' →
lead (pron: led)	thin strip of metal used to separate lines of type; made in standard thicknesses of 1pt, 1½pt, 2pt, 3pt, 6pt and 12pt
leader (pron: leeder)	1) in photography and cinefilm, blank film at beginning and end of roll or reel, used for threading to take-up spool 2) in printing, line of dots, thus . . . . used to take eye along line of type from one item to another
leading	action of inserting lead between lines of metal type to space them out; by extension, applied to 'line increment' → in photocomposition, but not recommended as being archaic
leaf	two backing pages of book
LED	initials of '*l*ight *e*mitting *d*iode': electronic display having same function as 'LCD' above, but with red characters on dark ground
left-handed coordinates (computer graphics)	'coordinate graph' → system involving depth dimension, denoted by 'z coordinate' → extending in this fashion:

legend	rather archaic synonym of 'caption' →
lens flare	in photography, tendency of camera lens to scatter light, especially from intense light source
lens-oriented	jargon adjective applied to areas of practice or study which include still photography, cinefilm and TV
letter assembly	catch-all term with same connotation as 'character assembly' → but less useful because less inclusive
letter fit	in type design, way in which characters are arranged to fit harmoniously with one another; better term would be 'character fit'
letter-quality printer (computers)	printout device capable of producing text of same quality as conventional typewriter

letter-spacing	inserting spaces between letters within word, as distinct from 'word-spacing' →: l e t t e r - s p a c e
letterpress	printing process in which impression is taken from raised surfaces of type matter or blocks; also called 'relief' or 'typographic' process:

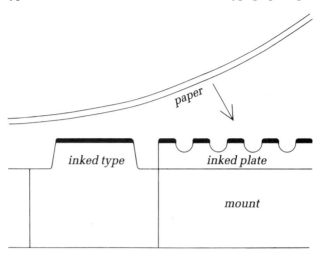

letterpress book	used by some to describe book which is printed (by whatever process) as distinct from 'stationery book'
letterset	rotary letterpress that transfers image from wraparound plate of offset cylinder, as with offset-litho (contraction of 'letterpress-offset')
LFO	initials of *l*ight-emitting *f*ibre *o*ptics
LG (of paper)	initials of '*l*ong *g*rain' →
lhp	abbreviation of '*l*eft-*h*and *p*age'
library binding	one of strength and durability suited to frequent handling of book over long period
library material	manuscript, typescript, typesetting or illustration matter retained on file for possible future use in publishing house
library shot	in cinefilm and TV, one from existing source, not specially taken
lifting	same as 'picking' →
ligature	two or three characters joined together as one (or more precisely the visible ink joining them), eg:

light box   one having translucent illuminated, usually by means of carefully colour-matched light source, for purpose of examining transparent material

light-fast ink   one which does not fade appreciably when exposed to light for long periods, as distinct from 'fugitive' ink

light pen (computers)   mobile, highly sensitive photoelectric attachment resembling pen, used with some VDTs to call up images from computer store by passing 'pen' over surface of screen; can also be used to change or adapt them:

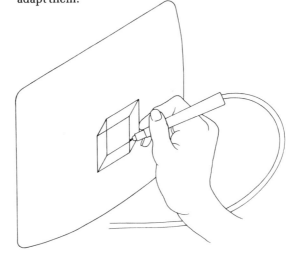

limp binding   one with flexible cover made of paper, cloth or plastic; usually called 'soft binding' or 'soft cover' in US

line-and-halftone plate   line and halftone images combined on one plate; known in US as 'combination plate' or 'combo'

line art   'artwork' → in line only; that is, without halftones

line-at-a-time printer (computer graphics)   same as 'line printer' →

line block   one which produces line result (ie: not halftone); called 'linecut' or 'line engraving' in US

line caster   typesetting machine that casts type as one whole line (slug) as against single-character caster

line conversion   transforming halftone original into line image by eliminating all middle tones; sometimes called 'drop-out' (but see 'drop-out half-tone')

line-endless tape (computers)   same as 'unjustified tape' → and 'idiot tape'; often (most confus-ingly), shortened to 'endless tape'

line feed	amount, measured in points or parts of point, by which direct impression and photocomposition machines advance paper or film from line to line; also known as 'film feed'
line-feed code	in photocomposition, instruction to 'photounit' → on type of line-feed required
line-for-line	instruction to typesetter to set in lines exactly as shown on original
line gauge	same as 'type scale' →; term more common in US
line graph	see 'coordinate graph'
line increment	in typesetting, smallest amount by which basic line interval may be increased; in hot metal typesetting this is ½ 'point' → but in photocomposition it may be as little as one-eighteenth of a point
line interval	vertical distance between base line of one line of type to base line of next; basic line interval corresponds to 'body size' of metal type but this phrase has no relevance for photocomposition and direct impression methods
line number	in photocomposition and computer print-out generally, numbering of each line as set, for correction location purposes
line original	one that is intended for line reproduction
line printer (computers)	output device, in form of drum, chain or CRT printer, which prints out whole line of characters at once, at speeds of 500–2,000 lpm (lines per minute); may be used in photocomposition to produce 'hard copy' for proof-reading
line segment (computer graphics)	in 'vector graphics' →, any line bounded by 'endpoints' →
-line type	method of size measurement for wooden type, one 'line' being 12 points
lineale	British Standards term for those typefaces otherwise known as 'sans serifs' →
linen finish	surface treatment, usually of covers, to simulate linen texture
linen tester	form of magnifying glass especially suited to examining dot-patterns of halftone reproductions in detail
lining figures	set of type numerals that line up with capitals thus: 1234567890 as distinct from 'old style figures' →; sometimes known as 'ranging figures' or 'aligning figures'
lining-up table	one with surface illuminated from below and with grid lines and/or moving scales superimposed, used to check accuracy of film positives and negatives, and back-up and register of proofs

Linofilm	trade name for photocomposition system of Linotype Paul (UK) and Mergenthaler (US)
Linotron	trade name for high-speed photocomposing system of Linotype Paul (UK) and Mergenthaler (US)
Linotype	obsolescent type composing machine that produces a line of type (slug) in one piece, similar to Intertype
linting	in offset lithography, accumulation of loose bits of uncoated paper on surface of blanket cylinder, affecting print quality
lip-sync	in cinefilm and TV, matching lip movements of speaker on film to sound recording of voice
liquid crystal display (computer graphics)	see 'LCD'
literal	spelling error due to wrong, or omitted, letter in typesetting; known as 'typo' (typographic error) in US
literary-minded	derogatory term applied by some graphic designers to others who show concern for such factors as readability
lith film	one that gives high definition and high contrast, cutting out middle tones, used for photomechanical reproduction
litho to gravure conversion	technique in which original stages of 'photomechanical process' → are as for litho, including variable area cells, but which is converted for gravure by engraving variable depths to cells in addition
lithography (abb: litho)	'planographic' → printing process (the commercial form of which is photolithography) in which surface of stone or metal is treated with chemicals so that some portions accept ink and some reject it:

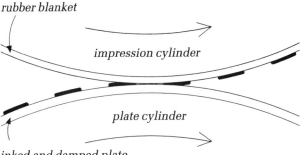

rubber blanket

impression cylinder

plate cylinder

inked and damped plate

live matter (type)	set matter intended for use, as distinct from 'dead matter'
liveware (computers)	rather dubious reference to human involvement in computer operations, as extension of 'hardware' → and 'software' → (see also 'wetware')

load (computers)	enter data
loading (of paper)	substance added to pulp of paper to improve opacity and allow high finish (eg: china clay)
LOC	initials of *l*etterpress to *o*ffset *c*onversion
loc cit	abbreviation for *loco citato*, Latin for 'in the place cited'; used in footnotes
local area network (computers)	one linking several output devices to same computer and output device, with arrangement to ensure that only one input device is on line at a time
locus	path described by point moving according to given law, eg: point moving at constant distance from second fixed point traces locus which is circular
log-off, logoff (computers)	signing at conclusion of interactive session
log-on, logon (computers)	identifying and authenticating oneself, usually by keying-in of 'password' →, when commencing operation
logarithmic graph	coordinate graph → in which vertical scale is arranged in logarithmic cycles rather than straight arithmetical progression:

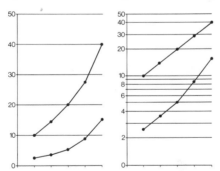

logic symbols	type characters used in symbolic logic are:
logical tree	simple form of 'algorithm' → showing choices or decisions available in given circumstances; broken down into sequence of 'yes/no' steps
LOGO (computers)	high level interactive computer language developed mainly for educational applications
logogram	sign or character standing for word
logotype (abb: logo)	letters or words forming distinctive whole, often used for trade name or brand name; originally, result of fusing two or three type characters on single type body (not necessarily as 'ligature')

long cross	same as 'dagger' →
long descenders	variants of typeface that have longer 'descenders' → than normal, eg:

10 PT.

When jobs have type sizes fixed quickly margins

10 (LONG DESC.) ON 12 PT.

When jobs have type sizes fixed quickly margins

long grain (of paper)	indication in specification or quotation for print that longer dimension of sheet runs with grain of paper (see 'machine direction')
long letters	those type characters that take up almost whole of body, eg:

Q ƒ

long 's'	type character used in printed English until early 19th century:

inſtruction *enſemble*

look-through	appearance of paper when viewed against light; also called 'see-through' in US
loop (computers)	sequence of instructions in program that is repeated until programmed precondition is fulfilled
loose-leaf	one which permits leaves to be removed at will; see also 'ring-binder', 'multi-ring binder', 'Wire-O binder', 'plastic comb/coil binder' and 'binding methods'
low key	photographic image in which, by lighting and/or processing, most of tones are very dark:

low level language (computers)	programming language that closely resembles numerical machine code, as against 'high level language'
low resolution scanning (computer graphics)	electron-beam 'raster scan' → producing 'pixel array' → of 512×512 or below
lower-case (abb: lc)	small letters in typeface (a, b, c, d) as distinct from upper case/caps and small caps
LPI, lpi	initials of *l*ines *p*er *i*nch
lpm	initials of '*l*ines *p*er *m*inute', rate at which 'computer output device' → will print out typed lines; slowest printers operate at about 20 lpm, fastest at about 4,000 lpm
LQ	initials of '*l*etter *q*uality' →
LSI	initials of *l*arge *s*cale *i*ntegration; see 'fifth-generation computers'
Ludlow	obsolescent type composing machine involving hand assembly of matrices and machine casting in 'slug' → form; used for newspaper headlines

M

M	abbreviation for 'mega-' →
m	abbreviation for 'milli-' →
m	in metric system, symbol for metre
M weight	US term for weight of 1000 sheets of specified size of sheet
MAC	acronym for *m*ulti-*a*ccess *c*omputing
machine code (computers)	low-level computer language devised to instruct machine in its arithmetical and editing functions without translation
machine composition	any operation producing type matter by means of keyboards and composing machines
machine direction (of paper)	same as 'grain direction' →
machine-finished paper	uncoated paper smoothed on both sides, but not as glossy as super-calendered paper

129

machine-glazed paper	uncoated paper polished to high gloss on one side but left rough on other; suitable for posters
machine minder	skilled printing operative who sets up printing press and tends it during print run; known in US as 'pressman'
machine plate	in lithography, one used for actual print run, as against 'proofing plate' →
machine proof	first copies off printing machine before it begins full run, used as final check proof
machine readable (computers)	of data in general, those which can be read into computer by punched tape, magnetic disc, etc; of alphanumeric sets, those which can be read by 'OCR' → and 'MICR' → encoding equipment
machine sheet	any printed sheet off printing press during run
machine word (computers)	not 'word' at all in conventional sense but unit of transfer located in 'memory' → of some machines containing pre-determined set number of 'digit positions' →, as against operating method in 'character-orientated' computers that use strings of digits varying according to program specification; typical machine word for most microprocessors is 'byte' → or two-byte unit of transfer
machining	printing operation relating directly to feeding sheets or webs (reels) onto press and making inked impression; may include other operations such as folding and trimming if these are executed on machine
macron	horizontal line over vowel indicating that it is 'long', thus: tēdious
macrophotography	photography of small objects by means of standard camera fitted with bellows extension or special lens extension tubes
mag	abbreviation of 'magnetic', as in 'mag tape'
magenta	red-blue colour containing no green; one of three primaries used in 'subtractive colour mixing' →
magnetic bubble memory (computers)	method of storing data as magnetic bubbles; single component can store over one million 'bits' of information – considerably more than comparable magnetic disk
magnetic disk (computers)	data storage device in form of disk to which signals are imparted within tracks on magnetized surface; there are three types, 'hard/rigid' →, 'floppy/diskette' → and (hard) 'mini-disk' →
magnetic drum (computers)	'magnetic medium' → in form of cylinder; has large data storage capacity suitable for attachment to 'central processor unit' →
magnetic ink characters	see 'MICR'

magnetic medium	any material coated with chemical on which data may be implanted as sequence of magnetized spots; typical forms of carriers are tape (reel or cassette), disk (floppy or rigid) and drum
magnetic track (of cinefilm)	alternative to 'optical track' →, using stripe of recording medium; increasingly used for projection systems, it will eventually replace optical sound track
main frame (computers)	vague colloquial reference to large-capacity computer, as contrasted with 'mini-computer' → and 'microcomputer' →
majuscules	upper-case characters, written or typeset
makeovers	US term for work and/or materials wasted in execution of printing work (UK term: spoilage)
make-ready	preparing printing surface on press, ready for printing
make-up	to arrange type matter, blocks and spacing material into pages
making	one complete batch of paper from mill; large printing companies often buy whole making for themselves
manifold	very thin 'bank' paper →, used when large number of carbon copies is required
manilla	strong, buff-coloured paper used for envelopes and folders, made from fibrous hemp
manual input unit (computers)	one designed for operator to enter data, usually by way of keyboard, without need of intermediate devices such as punched cards or paper tape
manuscript (abb: MS, pl: MSS)	any written matter intended for typesetting (also called 'copy'); more specifically, handwritten, as against typewritten copy
map projections (global)	see 'cylindrical projections', 'Mollweide's equal-area projection', 'Sanson-Flamsteed's equal-area projection' and 'zenithal projections'
marbling	staining paper to produce effect of marble grain; used mainly for endpapers, especially of account books
marching display	in photocomposition, narrow display unit attached to keyboard which shows about 30–40 of last characters keyed
margin-notched card	same as 'edge-notched card' →
mark-up	see 'type mark-up'
mark-up board (computers)	same as 'graphic tablet' →

mark-up language	code added to word processor at input stage so that output disk may be accepted by photocomposition system without need for complex conversion procedure
marked proof	one containing corrections, whether from printer's reader, publisher or author
market-led	term that, when applied to practice and teaching of graphic design, signifies cop-out to market 'research', poll-taking and similar mechanisms for eliminating any eccentric, intuitive or unpredictable concepts
married print	in cinefilm, finished print that has sound combined with picture on same film; also known as 'composite print'
mask	in word-processing, VDU display of standard blank form which is then filled in with data by operator; also used as synonym for 'flat' →
masking	adjusting light values in photomechanical processing, especially of colour; also used as synonym for 'scaling' → and 'cropping' →
master file (computers)	ambiguous term implying 1) stable collection of data that is drawn on routinely, or 2) current file that is regularly updated to incorporate records of new transactions
master proof	galley proof or page proof containing printer's corrections and queries, to which author's corrections are added and which is returned to printer
masthead	information about publishing house which appears above editorial of newspaper or on contents page of periodical; sometimes (inaccurately) used as synonym for 'nameplate' →
matchprint	trade name for popular make of 'dry colour proof' →
mathematical signs	some type characters used in mathematical settings are:

$+$ plus
$-$ minus
$\div$ divided by*   *   following are also valid:
$\times$ multiplied by** $^{234}/_{123}$ or 234/123
$=$ equal to   **   in algebra, following are also valid:
$\neq$ not equal to xy or $x\cdot y$ (ie: x multiplied by y)
$\equiv$ identical with
$\not\equiv$ not identical with
$\approx$ approximately equal to
$\simeq$ proportional to
∞ varies directly as
$>$ greater than
$<$ less than
$\geq$ equal to or greater than
$\leq$ equal to or less than
$\therefore$ therefore

∴	because *or* since
√	square root
∛	cube root
‖	parallel to
⊥	perpendicular to
→	approaches
↔	mutually implies
∞	infinity
Σ	sum of
Π	product of
∫	integral sign

matrice alternative spelling of 'matrix' →

matrix (general) womb: place where something is developed, formed; latterly, by extension, grid basis of tabular information

matrix, mat mould for casting type character in machine composition; also,
(character generation) 'image-carrier' → or 'image-master' → to photocomposition machine

matrix (mathematics) rectangular array of quantities in columns and rows, devised to obey specific rules and to assist in specific mathematical operations:

matrix printer computer output device producing characters composed from 'dot matrix' →:

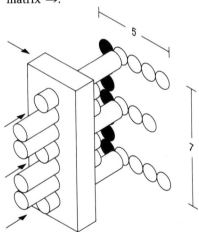

matt art 'coated paper' → with dull finish

matte in cinefilm and TV, mask used to blank off one part of negative during exposure to allow superimposition of another shot; 'travelling matte' involves shooting subject against plain blue background onto which is later imposed additional background scene (in TV this can be done simultaneously by electronic wizardry; known as 'colour separation overlay' or 'Chroma Key'

mb abbreviation of '*me*ga*b*yte' →

133

mean-line	upper limit of 'x-height' →: imaginary line running along tops of lower-case characters which do not have 'ascenders'; also known as 'x-line', especially in US
measure	width to which any line of type is set, usually expressed in 12pt (pica) ems; distinction may be made between maximum line length (measure) and other, lesser, line lengths within this measure
mechanical	same as 'camera-ready art(work)'; term commonly used in US, much less so in UK
mechanical binding	one in which leaves are fastened by inserting metal or plastic units into holes punched or drilled through them; may be permanent, as in spiral binding, or loose-leaf, as in ring binder (see 'binding methods')
mechanical pulp (UK)	basis of newsprint and other cheap printing papers made by mechanical, not chemical, process; known in US as 'groundwood'
mechanical tints	patterns of dots or lines which are laid down on prescribed areas of artwork; may be applied either before or during processing proper
medium (pl: media)	in communications industry, means whereby information is conveyed: book, movie, newspaper, radio, TV; last three are often grouped as 'mass media'
medium resolution scanning (computer graphics)	electron-beam 'raster scan' → producing 'pixel array' → of 1024 × 1024
mega-	prefix denoting one million (but see 'megabyte')
megabyte (computers)	literally means one million 'bytes' → but actually stands for 1,048,576 bytes, a 'binary million' or 2^{20}
memory, main memory (computers)	rather a misnomer but well established term for main data store of computer, available for immediate access by operator, as against 'backing store' →
menu (computers)	on-screen display of list of possible commands in interactive system
Mercator's projection	see 'cylindrical projections (global)'
merge (computers)	creation of single set or 'file' → of records by combining two or more existing files
Mergenthaler Linotype	internationally established manufacturers of Linotype, Linoterm, Linotronic, CRTronic and Linotron typesetting machines
Metafont (computer graphics)	computer program devised by Knuth at Stanford University by which means operator can specify and control digitized character set using appropriate choice of input parameters
metal halide lamp	photographic light source with rating up to 5,000 watts, consisting of

very small discharge seal encased in outer bulb; also known as 'compact-source iodide lamp'

metallic ink   printing ink containing fine powdered metals such as bronze, copper or aluminium

metric prefixes   these are:

micro– =	millionth	deca- =	ten times
milli- =	thousandth	hecto- =	hundred times
centi- =	hundredth	kilo- =	thousand times
deci- =	tenth	mega- =	million times

mf   initials of 'more follows'; inserted at foot of each page of newspaper copy except last one

MF (paper)   abbreviation for 'machine-finished' →

MG (paper)   abbreviation for 'machine-glazed' →

MICR   initials of 'magnetic ink character recognition'; use of special ink for machine reading of numerals and letters, especially for cheques and other banking applications, requiring special type designs:

E13B

CMC7

micro-opaque   microform record on opaque material, usually paper or card

microcomputer, micro   small desk-top machine based on 8-bit or 16-bit 'micro-processor' →, originally intended for single person use, thus differentiating it from 'minicomputer' →, but can now be equipped with operating systems for several simultaneous users; many desk-top word-processor and typesetting systems are based on microcomputers but others may require access to main-frame computer

microfiche   microform recording medium in which many images are arranged in rows on sheet of film, usually 6 × 4 in, and space is left for eye-legible title; there are various formats but those recommended by International Standards Organization are:

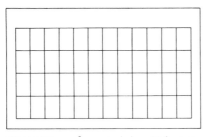

75 × 125mm format giving 48 images   *continued overleaf*

135

continued

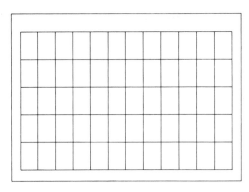

105 × 148mm format giving 60 images

microfilm   used in data processing and for documentation and record compilation; material is most often filmed onto 16mm ('cine' or 'comic' formats) for use as reels:

16mm 'cine' format   *16mm 'comic' format*

microfloppy   small 'floppy disk' → having diameter of less than 100mm (4in)

microform   generic term for all kinds of microrecording, whether opaque or transparent

micrographics   technique of reducing information photographically for compactness and convenience

microprocessor   electronic device consisting of tiny sliver of, typically, non-metallic silicon, a 'semi-conductor' →; functions as 'memory' → and instruction mechanism for central processing unit (CPU) in computer

middle/mid space   one of three standard word spaces in handsetting, ¼em of set; other two are 'thin' and 'thick' (see 'word spacing')

military projection   see 'oblique projections'

milking machine (computers)   slang for 'text retrieval terminal' →

mill ream   472 sheets of handmade or mould-made paper

millboard   hard, tough, well-rolled board with good finish; used for covers of account books and some case-bound printed books

milli-   prefix denoting one thousand

mimeography	popular name for stencil ink-duplicating process, derived from trade name Mimeograph
mini-disk (computers)	small 'hard disk' → that is now replacing 'floppy disk' → in some systems; can hold more data – 10–80 'megabytes' → – as compared to up to about 1.5 megabytes for floppy
mini-web	small 'web-offset' → press, typically printing in four colours, that is economical for shorter runs
miniature camera	see 'camera types'
minus leading	in photocomposition, reduction of space between lines of type to give line interval less than stated point size of type; unsuitable term, since 'lead' is not involved ('negative linespacing' is preferred)
minus letterspacing	reduced space between letters, or characters, beyond what is considered 'normal'
minus linespacing	same as 'minus leading' but not much better, as it is too cryptic
minuscules	lower-case characters, written or typeset
mirroring (computer graphics)	technique of drawing one half of symmetrical figure, then instructing computer to complete matching half (see also 'swept surface')
mix	same as 'dissolve' →
mm	in metric system, symbol for millimetre
MM Paper System	in US, attempt to standardize 'basis weight' → by relating substance to 1,000 sheets of 1,000 square inch area
mnemonic code (computers)	operator instructions in easily-remembered abbreviations, eg:

COM	*combine*
ESC	*escape*
FIL	*file*
HEL	*help*
PRI	*print*
SAV	*save*
SEL	*select*

mock-up	rough simulation of newspaper, periodical or book, showing intended position of type matter and illustrations
mode (computers)	one of two or more ways in which 'hardware' → devices or 'software' → programs may operate, such as 'binary mode', 'character mode', 'conversational mode' →

modem (computers)

acronym for *mo*dulator/*dem*odulator: device that adapts digital data from computer for transmission via analog channel such as telephone line, and converts signals sent along analog channel back into digital form; also known as 'data phone' and 'data set'

modern face

class of typeface dating from late 18th century, characterized by fine hairlines and unbracketed serifs:

moiré pattern

fancy way of describing 'screen clash' → but can best be applied to desirable use of this effect:

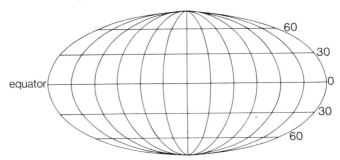

Mollweide's equal-area projection

global projection in form of ellipse in which equator is twice length of central meridian; projection is much improved by interrupting it through oceans:

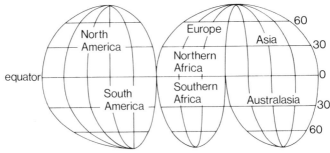

Mollweide's equal area

Mollweide's interrupted

monograph	publication dealing with single object or person
monoline (typeface)	one in which all letter strokes are equal thickness (or seem to be); may be either sans-serif or slab-serif:

ABCDefghIJKLmn

Monophoto	trade name for Monotype's photocomposition system
monorail camera	see 'camera types'
monospaced characters	text output, whether by manual, electrical or electronic means, in which all characters occupy same set width, as against 'proportional character spacing' →
Monotype	obsolescent system involving two machines (keyboard and caster) that produce metal type in single characters
montage	juxtaposition of two or more images so as to derive new meaning not present before; may be effected in space, as on a page, or in time, as in cinefilm (see also 'photomontage')
mordant	corrosive liquid used in 'etching' → and engraving generally
Morse code	alphabet invented by Samuel Morse in 1832 for transmitting telegraphic messages, using dots and dashes or long and short signals; since code is devised so that most commonly used vowels and consonants are represented by simplest grouping of dots and dashes, it makes most economical use of time and transmission power:

A ·—	N —·	1 ·————
B —···	O ———	2 ··———
C —·—·	P ·——·	3 ···——
D —··	Q ——·—	4 ····—
E ·	R ·—·	5 ·····
F ··—·	S ···	6 —····
G ——·	T —	7 ——···
H ····	U ··—	8 ———··
I ··	V ···—	9 ————·
J ·———	W ·——	0 —————
K —·—	X —··—	
L ·—··	Y —·——	
M ——	Z ——··	

mortised type	one which has part of body cut away to enable letter to fit closer; more common in larger sizes of ornamented wood types
mortising	in photocomposition, replacing portion of incorrect text by corrected version
mount	wood, metal or plastic base on which printing plate is fixed to bring it to type-height → for letterpress printing
mouse (computers)	hand-held input device with rollers on its base that record relative movements on any surface as digital increments as compared with 'tablet' →, that records absolute positions; usually contains several buttons used to input commands:

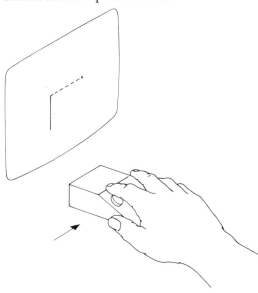

moving peg-bar	in film animation, 'peg-bar' → equipped with geared movement to achieve panning across field area of rostrum camera
Moviola	in cinefilm, trade name for popular make of 'editing machine' →
MPS	initials of *m*icro*p*rocessor *s*ystem
MPU	initials of *m*icro*p*rocessor *u*nit
Mr Roy G Biv	mnemonic for order of colours in visible part of 'electromagnetic spectrum' →: red/orange/yellow/green/blue/indigo/violet
MS (pl: MSS)	abbreviation for '*m*anu*s*cript' →
mull	in book production, net fabric fixed to back of book to assist in holding case to book
Müller-Lyer figures	pair of figures devised to demonstrate optical illusion; upper

140

horizontal appears longer than lower one but in fact both are same length:

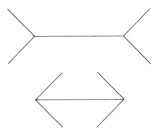

multi-access
(computers)

system permitting more than one user to interact with computer

multi-layer
microfiche

'microfiche' → having two layers of images using polarizing technique, or four layers using holographic technique; both intended to increase capacity beyond usual 98 'pages' of standard microfiche

multi-ring binder

ring binder with more elaborate mechanism (see 'binding methods')

multidisk reader
(computers)

device for reading many kinds of magnetic disks; useful for typesetting houses when accommodating clients' word-processing disks as input to their photocomposition systems

multiple exposure

in photography, exposing same image or different images on same film frame or same photoprint:

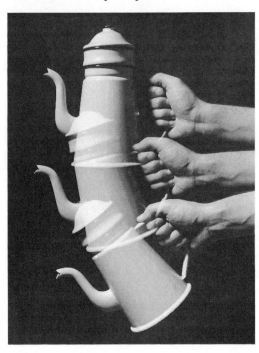

141

multiplexer (computers)	switching system enabling main computer to transfer data to several input/output devices simultaneously
multiview/ multiplane projections	'orthographic projections' → consisting of set of matched views of object, assembled as one drawing; views are best thought of as projected onto faces of glass box placed round object: two conventions exist: first angle projection (used in Europe and for building construction in UK) and third angle projection (used in US, Canada and for some engineering purposes in UK):

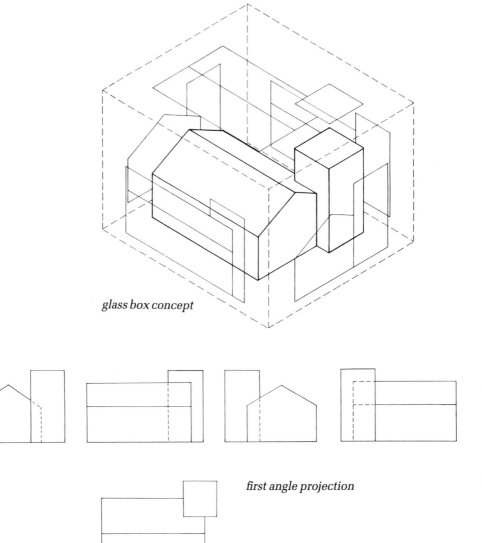

glass box concept

first angle projection

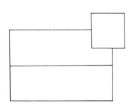

third angle projection

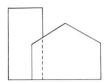 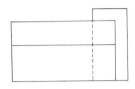  

mumping
(computers)

unauthorized, even piratical, transfer of data from one data store to another by means of devices such as 'text retrieval terminal' →

Munsell colour system

method of measuring colour which defines each colour according to three properties: 'hue' →, 'chroma' → and 'value' →:

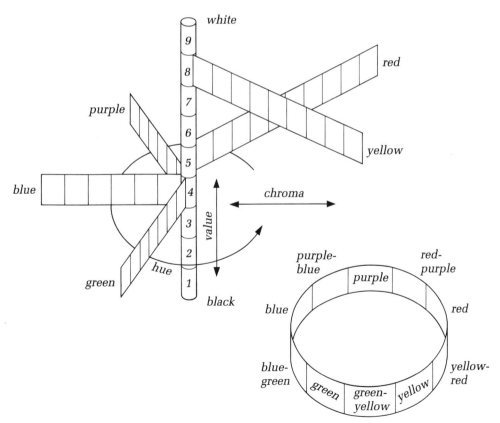

mute roll/neg/print	in cinefilm, one lacking sound track
mutton, mutt	familiar name of 'em-quad' →

N

n	in mathematics, symbol for indefinite number
nameplate (of newspaper)	title of newspaper in distinctive style, usually at top of page one, also known as 'flag'; sometimes incorrectly called 'masthead' →
nano-	prefix denoting one thousand-millionth or 10^{-9}
NAPLPS	initials of *N*orth *A*merican *P*resentation *L*evel *P*rotocol *S*tandard, relating to 'alphageometric' → display in 'videotex' → system
NBM	initials of *n*on-*b*ook *m*aterials
NBS	initials of US *N*ational *B*ureau of *S*tandards
NCGA	initials of (US) *N*ational *C*omputer *G*raphic *A*ssociation; rival body to 'SIGGRAPH' →
ncr	initials of *n*o *c*arbon *r*equired: trade name of form of stationery with special backing that performs same function as separate carbon interleaves
Necker's cube	one of several drawn figures used by perceptual psychologists to demonstrate visual ambiguity, pointed out by L A Necker in 1832; cube may be thought of as viewed either from above or below:

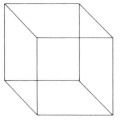

needle file	one using 'edge-notched cards' →
needle printer	same as 'matrix printer' →
negative line-feed	see 'reverse line-feed'
negative linespacing	in photocomposition, reduction of space between lines of type to give line interval less than stated point size of type; marginally preferred to 'minus leading' or 'minus linespacing' but still not recommended

network diagram	one representing nature of connexions between elements by means of 'nodes' ('vertices') and 'branches' ('arcs')
network identification	animated logotype or symbol screened regularly (and often infuriatingly) to proclaim identity of television broadcasting network
newsprint	cheap, absorbent, unsized paper used for newspapers
next reading/text/ editorial matter	instruction from advertiser in periodical, requiring that advertisement be positioned next to part of editorial content
nexus	from Latin verb 'to bind'; hence bond, link or point of interconnexion
nick (of type)	groove in shank of type →
nipping	in book binding, pressing text pages and case together to improve shape
NLP (computers)	initials of *n*atural *l*anguage *p*rocessing: technique of devising software to respond to commands in ordinary language
NLQ	initials of *n*ear *l*etter *q*uality: said of computer-driven laser printer with degree of resolution approaching that required for correspondence
node	from Latin *nodus*: point on stem of plant from which leaf springs; applied now to junction of paths in network
nominator	number above or in front of line in vulgar fraction; other number is 'denominator':

$$\frac{1}{3} \quad \textbf{1}\!\!/\!\!{3}$$

nomogram, nomograph	arranging three scales so that straight-edge joining known values on two scales is extended to third scale to provide desired value
non-counting keyboard	in photocomposition, input device which gives operator no information on which to base 'end-of-line decisions' →
non-impact printer	one that forms print image without touching surface; there are several types: 'electrostatic' →, 'electrothermal' →, 'ink jet' → and 'xerographic' →
non-destructive cursor (computer graphics)	in VDU display, one that can be moved around screen without automatically erasing or modifying data
non-lining figures	same as 'old-style figures' →
nonpareil (pron: nomprl)	name of old type size that approximated to 6pt; now used to describe 6pt lead

north point(er)	device used on plans and maps to give orientation; agreed form for this is:

notch binding	same as 'burst binding' →

np	initials of '*n*ew *p*aragraph', used in proof correction

ntm	initials of '*n*ext *t*ext *m*atter': request or instruction concerning placement of newspaper or periodical advertisement

NTSC	initials of *N*ational *T*elevision *S*ystem *C*ommittee, body responsible for standard of colour television broadcasting in North America and Japan; initials are used to identify standard itself

NTQ	initials of *n*ear *t*ypographic *q*uality: said of computer-driven laser printer with degree of resolution approaching that required for conventional printed work

numbering at/on press	applying number to each sheet during printing process rather than as separate operation

nut	familiar name for 'en-quad' →

O

obc	initials of '*o*utside *b*ack *c*over'

oblique projections	parallel projections → in which one face or object is parallel to plane of projection (picture plane) whilst visual rays (projectors) are inclined to plane of projection, as distinct from 'orthographic projections' →; there are three common types:

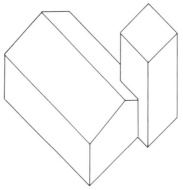

military (planometric): ground plane (plan) drawn parallel to plane of projection, vertical edges extended along inclined axis (usually, but not necessarily, 45°) at same scale or reduced scale

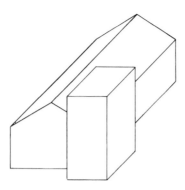

cavalier: front vertical plane (elevation) drawn parallel to plane of projection, receding edges extended along inclined axis at same scale

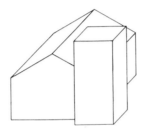

cabinet: as 'cavalier' but with receding edges drawn half-scale so as to give impression of fore-shortening

oblique roman

same as 'sloped roman' →; term more common in US

oblique stroke

see 'solidus'

OBR

initials of 'optical bar (code) recogniton' (see 'bar code')

OCR

initials of 'optical character recognition': using electronic scanner to read copy set on special typewriter, thus eliminating one stage of input; character set used must be acceptable to scanner:

ABCDEFG 12345678

(but note that increasing sensitivity in scanning is now rendering special OCR character sets obsolescent)

octal notation
(computers)

number system using 8 as 'radix' →, using digits 0 1 2 3 4 5 6 7, where each digit position represents power of 8; used to denote string of 'bits' → in computer (see also 'hex/hexadecimal notation')

octavo, 8vo

cut or folded sheet that is one-eighth of basic sheet size

offcut	paper cut to waste when sheet is trimmed to size; may sometimes be used for another print job
offline (computers)	said of any device not directly under control of central processor
offprint	feature or other portion of publication made available separately from whole work, especially for use of author; may be either 'run-on' of main printing or subsequent reprint (also known as 'separate')
offset photolithography, offset litho, offset	usual commercial form of photolithography, in which inked image is first transferred to rubber blanket, then to paper:

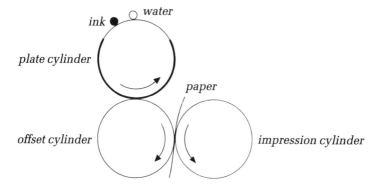

ogee	double curve that starts concave and becomes convex:

OK subject to correction	instruction on proof giving qualified go-ahead for printer to print, provided required proof correction has been made
OKWC	initials of *OK with corrections*: instruction to typesetter or printer to proceed to final setting or printing after corrections have been effected
old-face (UK) **old-style** (US)	class of typefaces dating from early 16th century:

ABC have work jobs

old-style figures	set of type numerals that includes some descenders, as distinct from 'lining figure' →: 1234567890

OLRT (computers)	initials of *on-line real time*, denoting an operating mode; see 'on-line' and 'real time'
on-demand publishing	increasingly used system, made much easier by computer control, whereby publication is printed on demand rather than being printed in large quantity and stored until needed
on-line (computers)	any operation in computer-controlled work which is directly connected to computer and any output matter resulting therefrom
on-line search (computers)	use of information retrieval system whereby operator interrogates computer on-line, eliciting series of responses that narrow search until suitable item of information is presented
on-the-fly printer (computers)	same as 'hit-on-the-fly printer' →
1/1	in specification for print, shorthand for: 'one colour (customarily black) printing on both sides of sheet'
one-point perspective	see 'perspective projections'
one-third reduction	amount to which 'half-up' → artwork is reduced in processing
onion skin	highly glazed, very thin, translucent paper
op cit	abbreviation for *opere citato*, Latin for 'in the work quoted'; used in footnotes
opacity	degree to which (a) ink will obscure colour of material on which it is printed, or (b) paper will prevent 'see-through' → or 'show-through' →
opaline	fine, translucent paper with high glaze, used for greeting cards
opaquing	blocking out portion of film negative to prevent reproduction of processing fault or unwanted part of image
open time	US term for time during print production cycle when nothing is happening (UK term is 'standing time')
optical (as noun)	in cinefilm and TV, any special effect such as wipe, freeze frame, dissolve and fade
optical alignment	arranging certain characters, such as T, to project into left-hand margin so as to give better appearance:

DON'T
TURN
BACK

optical brightener	fluorescent dye added to paper stock to make it 'brighter'
optical character recognition	see 'OCR'
optical coincidence card	same as 'peek-a-boo card' → and 'optical stencil card'
optical digital disk (computers)	one using laser to impart digital data onto track, to be 'read' by photoelectric sensor; similar to video but more versatile, offering random access to sound, picture, text and arithmetical data
optical fibre	extremely thin, flexible glass fibre, usually packed with others to form sturdy flexible cable; used to transmit information in form of light emissions for 'lasers' → and 'LEDs' →
optical printer	form of teletypewriter using cathode ray tube to project type character or line on sensitized surface to which black powder adheres; this is then transferred to paper
optical spacing	in typesetting, arranging letterspacing within line of caps to give more even effect; more correctly, 'optically even spacing':

OPTICAL SPACING

optical stencil card	same as 'peek-a-boo card' →
optical track	in cinefilm, normal method of incorporating sound on film by means of clear track of varying width running alongside image; see also 'magnetic track'
optical type fount	one intended for 'OCR' →
optical video disk	see 'video disk'
Oracle	trade name for UK Independent Broadcasting Authority's system for transmitting 'teletext' → news and information
orange peel	fault in 'lamination' → resulting in unpeeling at edges
ordinal numbers	first, second, third as distinct from cardinal numbers, one, two, three
ordinate	coordinate parallel to y-axis in 'coordinate graph' →
original (print)	copy, whether specially prepared or not, which is to be reproduced
origination costs	those arising from 'print origination' →
orihon	see 'zig-zag book'
ornament	see 'printer's ornament'

orphan	first line of paragraph appearing at foot of page; often considered undesirable
ortho-	prefix meaning 'straight', 'correct' or 'upright'
orthochromatic	applied to photographic film sensitive only to yellow, green and blue
orthographic projections	term used to cover those 'parallel projections' → in which visual rays are perpendicular to plane of projection (picture plane), as distinct from 'oblique projections' →
OSD	initials of *optical scanning device*
Ostwald system	method of measuring colour involving use of colour patch charts showing gradations of same 'hue' → from pure colour through progressive shading to black and progressive tinting to white; see also 'Munsell colour system'
out see copy	proof instruction directing printer to insert portion of copy that has been omitted
outboard computer	slang for one which is incorporated in device not connected on-line to large central computer and is confined to specific function
outer forme	one which includes outermost pages of folded section
out-of-house publisher	same as 'packager' → (term more common in US)
outline letter	one in which inner part has been removed, thus:

ABCDEFGHIJK

output devices (computers)	units designed to present information from computer, transcribed into suitable form for user; they include 'line printer' →, 'page printer' →, 'graph plotter' → and 'VDU' →
outsert	ghastly jargon for promotional item secured to outside of pack or periodical, in contrast to insert
outset	less common name for 'wrap-round' section →
outwork	printing operations that cannot be done by main printer and are sub-contracted out
over-matter, overset	typeset matter that cannot be accommodated within space allocated in newspaper, periodical or book
overhang cover	one which extends beyond trimmed leaves of book; may be either 'cased' or 'yapp' →

overhead projector	one which uses large transparent cels or rolls, either prepared or drawn direct, and an overhead lens that turns projected image through 90 degrees

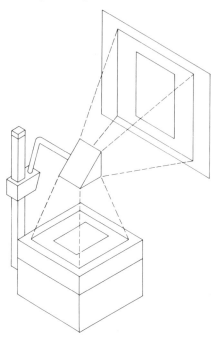

overlay	translucent or transparent material laid over piece of artwork or other original copy, on which instructions may be shown; also, one of series of separations in artwork drawn for colour reproduction
overprint	printed addition to job already printed
overs, overruns	any part of print run in excess of quantity ordered, usually by intention, to allow for 'spoils' →
overset	type matter that is set but not used
overstrike	operating typesetting or word-processing machine to produce special character by overstriking two standard characters, thus Y with – becomes ¥ (yen)
ozalid	trade name of 'diazo process' → used for photocopy proofs of direct impression or photocomposition settings, and of made-up pages

P

PA	initials of *p*aper *a*dvance: movement of paper through printer before next line of type is executed

packager	person or company that initiates and produces publication (usually illustrated) which is then acquired by orthodox publisher, under whose imprint it is distributed (also known as 'out of house publisher' in US)
packet switching (computers)	high-speed transmission of 'packets' of data so that several users may share same line
pad (computers)	see 'digitizing pad'
paddle (computers)	same as 'joystick' →
page	one side of leaf of book, subdivided thus:

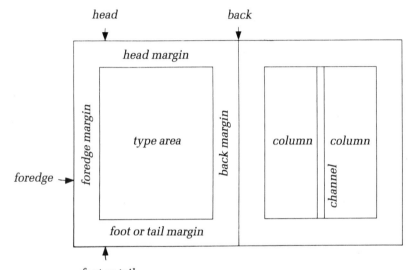

left hand page (lhp) or verso   right hand page (rhp) or recto

page (computers)	1) arrangement of computer-stored data into convenient working unit for system operations; 2) 'document' → or self-contained portion of it, which may or may not be accommodated in one 'frame' → of VDU screen; 3) one 'videotex' → display frame on screen, as part of some broadcast or dialup system
page-at-a-time printer (computers)	same as 'page printer' →
page description language	one devised to effect combination of text and pictures in composition of pages in desktop publishing and computer-controlled page make-up systems generally
page make-up terminal	in photocomposition, display device that gives view of keyboarded copy made up as whole page; some terminals offer facsimile of composed matter, others an approximation

page printer (computers)	output device in which character and line arrangement are pre-arranged, so that whole page is printed in one operation
page(d) proof	proof from print matter after it has been made up into pages
page turning (computers)	successive replacement of display 'pages' on VDU, either in set sequence or at choice of operator
Page View Terminal	trade name for one make of 'page make-up terminal' →
pages-to-view	number of pages appearing on one side of sheet; thus 16 page section would normally be '8 pages-to-view' (see also 'imposition')
paginate	to number pages of book consecutively (see also 'foliation')
pair kerning	see 'kerning pairs'
PAL	acronym for *P*hase *A*lternate *L*ine, one of two European standards for colour television broadcasting, both using 625-line; other is SECAM→
palette (computer graphics)	fixed set of colours offered by program for selection of desired colour by user
pan-and-tilt head	mounting attachment permitting camera (still or movie) to be rotated or tilted smoothly
panchromatic film	photographic film that is sensitive to the larger part of the visible spectrum, as contrasted to 'orthochromatic film' →
panning	1) in cinefilm and TV, rotating camera on mount during shooting, thus:

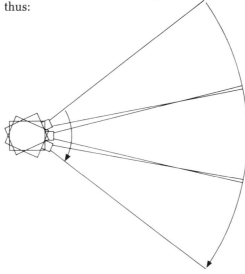

2) in interactive video graphics, moving image to left or right across screen

panoramic camera one with scanning lens that throws very wide image onto curved plate or film

pantograph device consisting of articulated rods, pointer and pen, used to copy any image to reduced or enlarged scale:

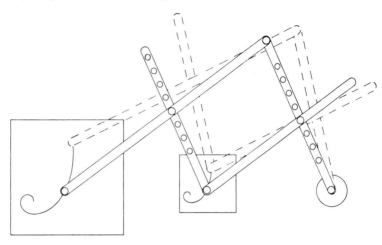

Pantone system trade name for colour-matching system covering inks, papers, pens and gouache; in specifying colour of printing ink, customer only needs to supply printer with reference number from specification book

paper master paper plate used in short-run, low-cost offset litho printing

paper sizes and subdivisions except 'A, B and C series of paper sizes' → traditional UK paper sizes derived from wide variety of independent needs and were not related rationally; most commonly used for printing were:

foolscap	13½ × 17in	these are 'broadsheet' sizes; double
crown	15 × 20in	and quad sizes are arrived at by
large post	16½ × 21in	doubling and quadrupling folio, 4to
demy	17½ × 22½in	and 8vo sizes by halving, quartering
medium	18 × 23in	and dividing by eight
royal	20 × 25in	

since 1970, UK printers, publishers and paper makers have agreed on following rationalization of untrimmed sheet sizes:

metric quad crown	768 × 1008mm
metric quad large crown	816 × 1056mm
metric quad demy	888 × 1128mm
metric quad royal	960 × 1272mm
RA0	860 × 1220mm
SRA0	900 × 1280mm

continued overleaf

155

continued

with these subdivisions for trimmed book sizes:

	quarto	octavo
metric crown	264 × 189mm	186 × 123mm
metric large crown	258 × 201mm	198 × 129mm
metric demy	276 × 219mm	216 × 138mm
metric royal	312 × 237mm	234 × 156mm
A4 297 × 210mm		
A5 210 × 148mm		

in US at time of writing there is no official rationalization of paper sizes, either trimmed or untrimmed, though moves have been afoot for some years to promote change over to metric standards, as has already been effected in Canada; meanwhile most commonly used (untrimmed) sheet sizes are:

23 × 35in, 25 × 38in, 26 × 40in, 28 × 44in, 32 × 44in, 36 × 48in and 38 × 50in

similarly, trimmed sizes for stationery, books and periodicals proliferate in US; among them the following have been identified:

4 × 9, 4¼ × 5⅜, 4¼ × 7*, 4½ × 6, 5¼ × 7⅝, 5½ × 7, 5½ × 8½, 6 × 9, 7 × 10, 8½ × 11†, 8¾ × 11½, 9 × 12, 9½ × 12⅜, 10½ × 13 and 11 × 13

*most common pocket book size
†most common stationery size, also most common periodical size

paper-to-paper see 'fold-to-paper'

paperless WP word-processing system that imparts alphanumeric images direct onto film, in full size or as microfilm, without intervening print on paper

paperback book with paper cover, also known as 'softback' or 'soft cover' and in US (if of small format) as 'pocketbook'

papyrus writing material made from pressed stalks of large reed; used in ancient Egypt, Greece and Rome

para- prefix meaning either 'beside' as in *para*llel, 'beyond' as in *para*normal or 'against' as in *para*sol

parabola 'locus, → of point that moves so that its distances from fixed point and from fixed straight line are always equal; see also 'conic sections'

paragraph mark type character indicating beginning of new paragraph, usually as alternative to indentation; also used as sixth order of 'reference marks' →

parallax error in photography, difference between what is seen through viewfinder

156

and what is recorded on film, especially evident in twin-lens reflex camera:

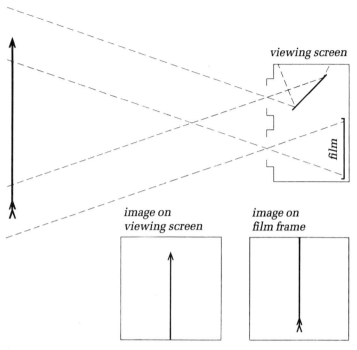

viewing screen

film

image on viewing screen

image on film frame

parallel
type character used as fifth order of 'reference marks' → for footnotes

parallel fold
folding sheet once, then again along line parallel to first fold (see 'folding methods')

parallel projections
drawing projections in which observer is considered to be at infinity, so that 'visual rays' (also called 'projectors') are parallel to each other; see also 'perspective projections', 'oblique projections' and orthographic projections:

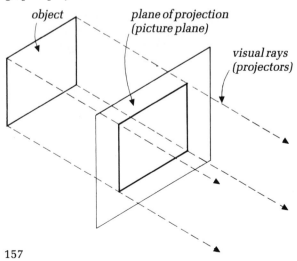

object

plane of projection (picture plane)

visual rays (projectors)

parallel rule / **straightedge**	drawing instrument consisting of straightedge controlled by pulley system that keeps it horizontal whilst permitting movement up and down
parameter	variable quantity given fixed value for any one specific calculation; often misused as synonym for 'limit'
parchment	animal skin, typically of sheep or goat, prepared for manuscripts
parentheses	see 'brackets'
pars pro toto	Latin for 'the part standing for the whole'; common device in graphic communication
Pascal (computers)	'high-level language' → derived from ALGOL; block-structured to enable employment of cycles, loops and selections
pass	one cycle of operation through printing or photocomposition machine; may involve more than one impression or transfer of image
passim	Latin for 'here-and-there'; used in footnotes
passive terminal (computers)	one that is not 'interactive' →
pass-on rate	in newspaper and periodical publishing, estimate of number of readers per copy
password (computers)	identifying set of characters keyed in by would-be user to verify right of access to machine
paste-up	any copy prepared for reproduction which comprises several elements assembled and pasted up as one; in addition, may refer to layout assembly used as guide to printer, not for reproduction
pasting in/on	same as 'tipping in/on' →
patch (computer)	instruction added to routine in order to correct error
patent	licence guaranteeing exclusive rights to inventor of 'any manner of new manufacture and any new method or process of testing applicable to the improvement or control of manufacture'
pattern recognition (computers)	facility built into some computers that recognizes specific features of input in order to identify, group or classify; typical features would be those detected by 'OCR' → and 'MICR' →
PBA	initials of *P*ublishers' *B*arcoding *A*ssociation
PC	initials of '*p*ersonal *c*omputer' →
PCMI	initials of '*p*hoto-*c*hromic *m*icro-*i*maging', relatively new 'microform' process capable of reduction ratios up to 200×

PE initials of '*p*rinter's *e*rror', indication on proof that error is made by typesetter and does not originate from author; US convention not common in UK (see also 'AA')

PE paper see 'resin-coated paper'

peculiar same as 'special sort' →

peek-a-boo card index one composed of 'feature cards', each of which contains an identical array of code numbers but which have varying patterns of holes punched to denote particular features, or 'descriptors', of subject:

peg-bar in film animation, device for holding film cels in register by means of shaped holes in cels which fit over 'pegs' or 'pins' in thin metal strip (see 'rostrum')

pel acronym of '*p*icture *el*ement' →

pen plotter (computers) one producing line drawings on paper or film under computer control

pentagon five-sided figure (see 'regular polygons')

pentagram five-pointed star formed by extending sides of pentagon, thus:

pentaprism in photography, five-sided prism that converts image on ground glass screen of reflex camera to right way round and right way up

perfect binding   binding method → in which cut backs of leaves of books are secured by synthetic glue; also known as 'threadless binding' or 'unsewn binding'

perfecting   printing second, or reverse, side of sheet; also called 'backing up'

perfecting press,   'rotary press' → that prints both sides of paper in one pass through
perfector   machine (though not simultaneously)

perforating at press   using sharpened, slotted rule locked into forme to produce dot or dash perforation in sheet

period   common US term for 'full point'

peripheral (as noun)   any device connected to computer which is not part of its central
(computers)   processor unit (CPU)

persistence   in 'CRT' →, characteristic of phosphor screen whereby image
(computers)   imparted by electron beam is visible for period after signal has ceased, though with diminishing strength

personal computer   'microcomputer' → of greater sophistication, including larger 'memory' and more functions than 'home computer' →; abbreviated as 'PC' →

perspective   drawing projections in which observer is considered to be stationed
projections   at finite point, as distinct from 'parallel projections' →:

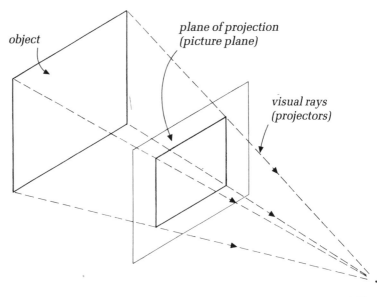

one-point perspective

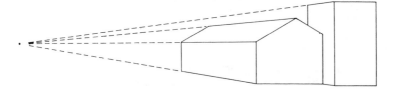

two-point perspective

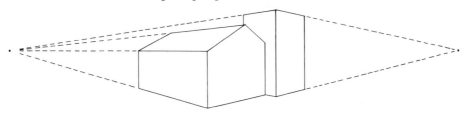

three-point perspective

161

PERT	acronym for '*P*rogramme *E*valuation and *R*eview *T*echnique': method of network analysis with close similarities to 'CPA/CPM', → with which it is now practically synonymous
petal printer	same as 'daisy wheel printer' →
PFK (computers)	initials of '*p*rogrammed *f*unction *k*eyboard': input device, generally used for entering commands or making choices relating to graphics programs, as against conventional alphanumeric text keyboard
pH	symbol denoting degree of acidity or alkalinity in any given substance according to scale 0–10; 0 = maximum acidity, 10 = maximum alkalinity
philoxenic	pseudo-Greek synonym for 'user-friendly' →
phonogram	written symbol representing spoken sound
phosphor	fluorescent substance used to coat inside of cathode ray tubes and fluorescent lamps
phosphor bloom (electronics)	in any phosphorescent display involving electron bombardment, tendency of phosphor's light to spread beyond area being bombarded
photocomposition	preferred term for any system of typesetting by photographic means, also known as 'phototypesetting' and inaccurately as 'photosetting' (but see also 'filmsetting'); photocomposition machines have developed through four stages, or generations: *first generation* those designed in close imitation of hot-metal machines *second generation* those using electromechanical systems which control mirrors, escapements and lenses *third generation* those generating type characters by means of cathode ray tubes *fourth generation* those involving use of lasers for exposure of image onto film or paper
photocopy	photographic copy from original; 'photostat' is one kind of photocopy
photodirect lithography	process using plates made direct from original artwork without intermediate (negative) stage
photodisplay unit	same as 'photoheadliner'
photoengraving	photomechanical etching process which produces a letterpress line or halftone plate
photoflood lamp	photographic light source similar in shape and size to ordinary domestic lamp but about 2½–3 times brighter
photogelatin process	another name for 'collotype' →

photogram	photographic image created without use of camera or film, by exposing photographic paper to light and throwing shadows on it:

photogravure	photomechanical 'intaglio' → printing process in which impression is taken from pattern of recessed dots (cells) of varying depth:

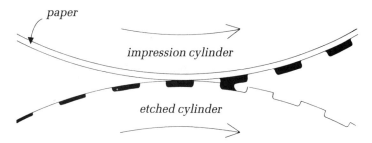

photoheadliner	machine producing display type by photographic means: letter-spacing may be either automatic or manual, and many makes have special lenses for condensing, expanding, slanting and otherwise distorting letter forms
photolitho(graphy)	photomechanical version of 'lithography' →; see also 'offset'
photomechanical	same as 'film assembly' →

163

photomechanical process	general term covering whole activity of converting original material in reproducible form (eg: printing plates) by photographic, chemical and mechanical means
photomechanical transfer	process particularly suited to rapid production of line photoprints for paste-up artwork; see also 'PMT'
photomontage	juxtaposition or superimposition of photographic images so that new meaning or impression is drawn from their combination, eg:

photonics	same as 'fibre optics' →
Photopake	trade name for opaque paint used for blocking out process negatives
photopolymer plate	flexible plastic printing plate made for use on 'rotary letterpress' →, 'belt press' → or in 'flexography' →
photoprint	used in photocomposition to describe equivalent of repro proof in machine composition
photosetting	vague term best avoided, but used to embrace all machines producing reproduction proofs of type images, whether for display or text matter, on film or paper
photostat, stat	trade name, now accepted as general, for thin photocopy used as part of paste-up layout or presentation visual
photostatic printing	see 'xerography'
phototelegraphy	see 'wire-photo'
phototype	another name for 'collotype' →

164

phototypesetting	alternative term for 'photocomposition' →
photounit	output component of photocomposition machine which does typesetting and production of phototype
pi	letter of 'Greek alphabet' → used as mathematical symbol for ratio of circumference of circle to diameter: 3.142 approx
pi characters	US term for 'special sorts' or 'peculiars', now in use in UK due to importation of US photocomposition machines
pi position	blank space or location in photocomposition systems provided so that users may insert special characters (pi characters) of their own choice
PIA	initials of Printing Industries of America
pic (pl: pix)	journalist's slang for photograph (picture)
PICAŞO (computer graphics)	graphics software package devised for use with 'FORTRAN' →
pica (typewritter)	larger of the two commonest typewriter faces →
pica, pica em	12pt em, standard unit of typographic measurement for type line length and spacing, 4.216mm (0.16604in); loosely known as 'em' in UK, so that when referring to aspects of type specification such as 'indent' → that is not in picas, it is best to specify '– ems of set' (see also 'IBM pica')
pica gauge/rule	same as 'type scale' →
pick (computers)	lighter, more delicate form of 'light pen' →
picking	break up of small portions of paper surface during printing, caused by tackiness of ink; also known as 'pulling' or 'plucking'
pictogram, pictograph	pictorial sign; that is, one resembling the thing it stands for:

picture description instruction (computers)	code used in composition of VDU image by combining lines, curves and shapes from keyboard

165

picture dragging (VDU)	moving displayed picture, or portion of it, to another part of screen
picture element (VDU)	see 'pixel'
picture plane	same as 'plane of projection' →
pie/pi (UK/US)	printer's term for metal type which has become mixed by accident
pie graph/chart	one in which proportions of whole are represented as slice segments of circular pie; also known as 'divided circle' and 'wheel graph':

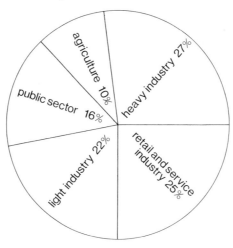

piece accent (US)	see 'floating accent'
piece fraction	in typesetting, fraction made up from more than one piece of type; also known as 'split fraction'
pin feed	method of offering continuous stationery paper to machine by locating pins on machine into lines of holes in paper
pin matrix	same as 'dot matrix' →
pin register	method of ensuring exact location of image-carrying material, whether opaque or transparent, by means of punched holes in image carrier corresponding to set of pins in frame
pincushion distortion	typical distortion in CRT image:

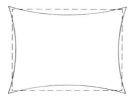

PIRA	acronym for UK *P*aper, *P*rinting and *P*ackaging *I*ndustries *R*esearch *A*ssociation
pitch	in typewriting, measure of number of characters accommodated within one inch of typing; usually ten characters per inch (10-pitch) or twelve (12-pitch)
pixel	acronym for 'picture element': small units or 'observations' comprising 'raster display' →
pixel array (computer graphics)	method of measuring degree of resolution in electron-beam 'raster scan' → display, expressed as A × B, where A is number of horizontal 'pixels' → and B is number of vertical pixels; see 'high resolution scanning', 'medium resolution scanning' and 'low resolution scanning'
PL/1	abbreviation of *P*rogramming *L*anguage 1, 'high-level language' → combining features of 'ALGOL' → and 'COBOL' →
plane of projection (abb: PP)	in 'parallel projections' and 'perspective projections' →, imaginary plane (usually vertical) interposed between object and 'station point', onto which image of object is projected; also known as 'picture plane'
planer	traditional term for wood block used to tap down type matter in place on letterpress 'stone' →
planning table	same as 'lining-up table' →
planographic	said of printing process such as lithography, in which printing surface is neither raised (relief) nor incised (intaglio)
planometric projection	see 'oblique projections'
plasma panel display (computers)	device that generates image by running electric current through series of gas-filled cells, each one of which performs as 'picture element' →; neater (because flatter) alternative to cathode ray tube display but with lower resolution
plastic comb/coil binding	see 'binding methods'
plate (in book)	illustration on different paper from that used for text
plate (printing)	metal, rubber or plastic surface from which impression is taken
plate camera	see 'camera types'
plate cylinder	in 'offset photolithography' →, one which carries inked plate, as against 'blanket cylinder'
plate finish	highly polished surface applied to paper by means of 'calenders' →

167

platen press	letterpress machine in which paper is pressed onto type matter from flat surface called a platen; one which has flat impression as distinct from cylindrical one:

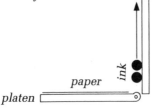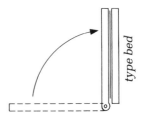

plot (as verb)	draw line to connect points on graph
plotter (computers)	see 'graph plotter'
plucking	same as 'picking' →
plus letterspacing	additional space between letters, or characters, beyond what is considered 'normal'
PMS	initials of '*P*antone *M*atching *S*ystem'; prefix attached to colour samples and specifications which employ that system
pochoir	French for 'stencil'; applied to use of that method as printing process
PMT (photoprint)	trade mark made from abbreviation for '*p*hoto*m*echanical *t*ransfer' → paper marketed by Kodak
pocket envelope	one with opening and flap on shorter side, as distinct from 'banker envelope':

pocketbook	'paperback book' → small enough to fit into pocket (term more common in US)
POCS	initials of US *P*atent *O*ffice *C*lassification *S*ystem
point (Anglo-American)	basic unit of typographic measurement: 0.351mm (0.013837in); 12 pts = 1 pica em
point	US term for one thousandth of an inch as applied to thickness of board
point (Didot)	equivalent to Anglo-American point, used in most European countries: 0.375mm (0.0148in); 12 Didot points = one cicero or *corps douze*

point mode (computers)	form of VDU display using dots to build image
polar chart	same as 'circular graph' →
polarizing filter	in photography, one used mainly to get rid of unwanted reflexions from water, glass and polished surfaces; may also be used to darken blue skies in colour photography
Polaroid	trade name for self-developing photographic materials and special equipment they require; process was invented in 1947 by Edwin Land and is variant of 'DTR' → process
Polaroid back	special holder fitted to conventional camera to hold Polaroid film
polygon	see 'regular polygon'
polygon mesh (computer graphics)	set of 'polygons' → connected edge-to-edge to form complex planar surface; typical method of simulation in computer-generated modelling:

POP	initials of 'Post Office Preferred'; range of envelope and postcard sizes recommended by UK Post Office, which include ISO envelope sizes DL and C6 (see 'A, B and C series of paper sizes')
POP-2 (computers)	'high-level language' → with applications to 'artifical intelligence' →
pop-on	in film animation, instantaneous appearance of new image in existing scene
pop-up menu (computer graphics)	'menu' – that is called up by means of key or button and disappears when selection has been made; also known as 'pull-down menu'
population pyramid	see 'pyramid graph'
portrait format	describes proportion of film, photoprint, artwork or any piece of print matter in which height is appreciably longer than width
POS	abbreviation of 'point-of-sale'

pos, pozzy	slang for 'positive transparency', with particular reference to those used in platemaking process
positional notation	form of numbering in which position of digit in row gives it significance in addition to its value; thus in normal decimal notation, ech row to left represents increase by factor of ten (see also 'octal notation' and 'hexadecimal notation')
post binder	see 'binding methods'
post sync	in cinefilm, recording sound to match image after shooting
postal trap	any mailed piece (eg: unsealed envelope) which may trap another during collection, sorting or delivery
posterization	separating range of tones in continuous-tone original into flat, graded tones, using several negatives, one for each grade, then making composite print of them all; also called 'tone separation':
postlims	see 'end-matter'
Postscript	trade name of popular 'page description language' →
pothooks	curved terminals of some type characters, especially in italics:

frjcag

p, pp	abbreviation for 'page', 'pages'
PP	abbreviation for '*picture plane*' →
PPI	initials of '*pages per inch*': measure of 'bulk' → of paper or board (term more common in US than in UK)
pragmatics	see 'semiotic(s)'
precedence key	method of extending effectiveness of standard 'QWERTY' → keyboard in which preliminary use of special key changes function of certain standard keys
preferred position	in periodical and newspaper publishing, an advantageous position for advertisements, such as one facing important editorial page; usually costs more
prelims	short for 'preliminary pages', those pages of book preceding main body (see also 'end matter'); following sequence is offered as

170

reasonable but not immutable:

half- (or bastard) title *recto*
list of other works by same author or in same series *verso*
frontispiece *verso* (could face any *recto* in prelims)
title *recto*
bibliographical note and imprint *verso*
dedication and / or quotation (epigraph) *recto*
preface / foreword *recto* or *verso* (or after contents)
acknowledgements *recto* or *verso* (or in end-matter)
list of contents *recto*
list of illustrations *recto* or *verso*
introduction *recto* or *verso* (may be considered as part of main text)

pre-make-ready   in printing, all those operations carried out on formes or printing plates to reduce time spent making ready on machine, eg: register checks, 'interlays' →

pre-press proof   one that is taken from any work that is to be printed, before the platemaking stage, eg: photoprint from process film

preprint   part of publication printed before main production, usually as loose sheet intended to be dropped into bound copies

presensitized plate   lithographic printing plate having sensitized coating already applied by machine

presentation visual   careful representation which may be drawn, photoprinted, typeset or an amalgam of these, to show intended effect of printed job; known in US as 'comprehensive' or 'comp'

press proof   last proof to be read before giving an OK to print

pressure bar / slide   same as 'plastic grip / slide binder' (see 'binding methods')

pressure-sensitive   used to describe 'transfer lettering' →

Prestel   trade name of UK Post Office's 'Viewdata' → service

preview screen   in photocomposition, 'VDU' → that shows view of composed work as it will appear when printed

primary colours   those from which all other colours may be mixed, ie: red, blue, green for 'additive colour' → and red-blue (magenta), blue-green (cyan), yellow for 'subtractive colour mixing' → it is best to refer to these as 'additive primary colours' and 'subtractive primary colours', to avoid confusion

primitive
(computer graphics)   basic elements in 'vector display' → program, such as 'line segments' → and 'endpoints' →, that can be manipulated by operator to compose screen images

print drum / barrel   that part of 'drum printer' → that contains engraved 'character set' →

171

print origination	preparatory work of print job up to proofing stage
print run	action of printing prescribed quantity of copies; quantity itself
print to paper	instruction to printer to use all available supply of paper rather than precisely specified number of copies
print wheel	same as 'daisy wheel' →
printability	degree to which an original, material or other intended component will contribute to an effective piece of print
printer-plotter (computers)	one that can produce simple graphic output as well as text
printer's flower	type ornament in form of small flower or plant:

printer's ornament	generic term covering all type matter intended to create decorative effects, such as borders, arabesques and flowers
printer's reader	one who corrects proofs at printer's before they are sent to author
printer's terms and conditions	cunning network of escape clauses, set in 3pt type and printed in invisible ink on reverse of printer's estimate
printing down	using 'vacuum frame' → to transfer image from one film to another (positive-negative, negative-positive) or to transfer film image onto printing plate
printing-down frame	same as 'vacuum printing frame' →
printing processes	fall into five main classes: those in which impression is taken from raised portions of surface (relief printing), those in which impression is taken from recesses in surface (intaglio printing), those in which impression is taken from flat surface treated chemically (planographic printing), those in which impression is made through stencil, and those in which no impression is involved

examples of these classes are:

relief	*intaglio*
woodcut	metal engraving
linocut	etching
letterpress	gravure

planographic	*stencil*
lithography	screen
collotype (photogelatin)	pochoir
hectography (gelatin duplicating)	ink duplicating (mimeograph)

172

no impression
photostatic (xerography)*
electrophotographic
ink-jet
thermal
*this process involves contact but not pressure

printmaking	any fine-art reproduction process, usually etching, woodcut, wood or steel engraving, or silkscreen
printout	computer output via 'teleprinter' →, 'line printer' → or 'graph plotter' →; printout may be either alphanumeric or graphic
pro-forma	invoice or statement rendered before supply of goods or services, usually to meet budget deadline
process camera	one constructed especially for photomechanical reproduction processes; also called 'graphic arts camera'
process engraving	making letterpress printing plate by printing down photographic image onto plate and etching to form relief printing surface
process inks	those used in 'four-colour' and 'three-colour process' →
process white	gouache specially made for use in artwork for reproduction
production run	main operation of machine, as against test run or pilot run
program (computers)	set of instructions devised to tell computer how to execute work
programmable function key (computers)	'function key' → which can perform different functions according to program in operation
programmed function keyboard (computers)	auxiliary device for inputting user commands, usually having 16 or 32 keys
progressives (abb: progs)	series of proofs showing each plate of colour set in sequence, individually and in registered combination
PROM (computers)	acronym for *p*rogrammable *r*ead-*o*nly *m*emory: type of 'ROM' → whose contents can be altered by user; see also 'EPROM'
prompt (computers)	question, guidance or instruction directed at operator from computer
Pronto	trade name for keyboard consisting of eight keys, five for character/ symbol selection and three 'shift keys' → ; intended for one-handed operation
proof	any preliminary impression from composed type matter or plates, for purpose of checking or revising before printing; but see also 'repro proof'

173

proof correction marks (UK) — these may be used for copy mark-up where appropriate

explanation	mark in text	margin mark	as corrected
delete/take out	tooøthache	♂	toothache
substitute letter	toøthache	o/	toothache
substitute word	~~lover~~	husband/	husband
insert letter	dreaⱱboat	m∧	dreamboat
insert period	finished∧	⊙/	finished.
insert space	getⱱout	Y/	get out
insert hyphen	rightⱱhanded	⊢⊣/	right-handed
insert comma	noⱱI will not	,∧	no, I will not
insert apostrophe	no I wonⱱt	⸳/	no I won't
insert superior figure	a⟨× b	²/	a² × b
insert inferior figure	HⱱSO₄	/₂	H₂SO₄
insert quotation marks	∧so-called∧	⁶⁶ ⁹⁹	'so-called'
set in lower case	myⓃame	≠/	my name
set in capital	<u>my</u> name	≡/	My name
set in italic	do it <u>now</u>	⊔⊔/	do it *now*
change italic to roman	(*stand up*)	⊔⊣/	stand up
set in bold	never again	⌇⌇⌇/	**never** again
set in small caps	Peter speaks	=/	PETER speaks
change small caps to lower case	(SAVE TIME)	≠/	save time
wrong fount; replace	anyhow	⊗/	anyhow
replace character	ⓟerhaps	x/	perhaps
transpose	we|ready|are|	⌐/	we are ready
let it stand as it is	up ~~the~~ junction	⊘/	up the junction
indent one em	But for him	⌐ 1em/	But for him
indent two ems	But for him	⌐ 2ems/	But for him
straighten	out of <u>whack</u>	=/	out of whack
equalize spaces	do|it|now|please	Ⅺ/	do it now please
close up	extraⱱpolate	⌒/	extrapolate
reduce space between characters	y|e|s	↑/	yes
reduce space between words	ah ↑ yes	↑/	ah yes
insert space between characters	yⱱes	Y/	y e s
insert space between words	ahⱱyes	Y/	ah yes
enclose in parentheses	∧he whispered∧	(/)/	(he whispered)
enclose in brackets	∧omitted∧	[/]/	[omitted]
include item overlooked	youⱱme	amaze∧	you amaze me
start new paragraph	after all.⎴Next	⌐/	after all. Next
run on	to him. ⌐ What for?	⊂⌐/	to him. What for?

the above marks correspond with those recommended in BS 5261:1976

proof correction marks (US)

these may be used for copy mark-up where appropriate

explanation	mark in text	margin mark	as corrected
delete/take out	tooȼthache	ℯ	toothache
substitute letter	toȼthache	o	toothache
substitute word	~~lover~~	husband	husband
insert letter	dreaᵦboat	m	dreamboat
insert period	finished‸	⊙	finished.
insert space	getᵦout	#	get out
insert hyphen	rightᵦhanded	=/	right-handed
insert comma	noᵦI will not	⌃	no, I will not
insert apostrophe	no I wonᵦt	ⱽ	no I won't
insert superior figure	aᵦ× b	²∕	a² × b
insert inferior figure	HᵦSO₄	∕₂	H₂SO₄
insert quotation marks	ᵦso-calledᵦ	ⱽ ⱽ	'so-called'
set in lower case	my N̸ame	ℓc	my name
set in capital	my name	cap	My name
set in italic	do it now	ital	do it *now*
set in bold	never again	bf	**never** again
set in small caps	Peter speaks	sc	PETER speaks
wrong font; replace	anyhow	wf	anyhow
replace character	⦶perhaps	X	perhaps
transpose	we│ready│are│	tr	we are ready
let it stand as it is	up ~~the~~ junction	stet	up the junction
indent one em	]But for him	▢	But for him
indent two ems	]But for him	▭	But for him
straighten	out of whack	=	out of whack
equalize spaces	do it now please	eq #	do it now please
close up	extra⌢polate	⌒	extrapolate
enclose in parentheses	ᵦhe whisperedᵦ	( )	(he whispered)
enclose in brackets	ᵦomittedᵦ	[ ]	[omitted]
include item overlooked	youᵦme	out, see copy	you amaze me
start new paragraph	after all. ⌈Next	¶	after all. Next
run in	to him.⌐ ⌊What for?	no ¶	to him. What for?

---

proof reader — any person who reads proofs for purpose of checking or revising before printing

proof reader's marks — agreed set of signs used by editors, proof readers and others concerned with copy preparation and proof correction

proofing plate in lithography, one made solely for proofing purposes; may be identical to actual printing plate ('machine plate') but could be specially made up for 'scatter/random proofs' →

proofing press one used for making proofs rather than making print runs; usually small machine not made for fast, prolonged runs

proportional dividers device for enlarging or reducing dimensions for drawings, or making conversions such as feet to metres

proportional scale simple device for scaling photo and artwork (see 'scaling'):

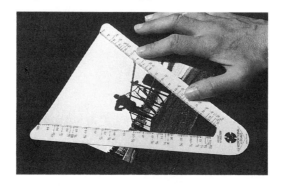

proportional typewriter one that spaces characters proportionally, so that 'i' occupies less width than 'w', for example; typewriters used for 'direct impression' → composition are almost without exception proportional

proto- prefix meaning 'original' or 'first' as in 'prototype'

protocol converter (computers) device that converts control codes used in one system so that they can activate another, as between 'word processor' → and 'photocomposition' → machines

protractor drawing instrument for measuring angles:

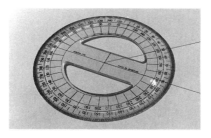

proud type matter standing away from general body of matter on page is said to be 'proud' or 'standing proud'

prove 'to prove' is to make a proof

pt in typesetting, abbreviation for 'point' →

PTW	initials of '*p*ersonal *t*ypesetting *w*orkstation'
publisher	one who sponsors and/or produces and/or distributes books to booksellers or direct to public; said by some to behave as impoverished gentleman when dealing with printer and as ruthless businessman when dealing with author
publisher's reader	one who reads and reports to publisher on submitted manuscripts
publisher's ream	one containing 516 sheets; also known as 'perfect ream'
puck (computers)	alternative name for type of 'stylus' → for use with 'digitizing pad' →
puff	slang for favourable editorial comment in newspaper or periodical, usually tied in with paid advertisement
pull	same as 'proof' →
pull-down menu	same as 'pop-up menu' →
pull-out	same as 'fold-out' →
pull-out section	portion of periodical intended to be pulled out; not necessarily complete 'section' in technical sense (could be centre 4pp of 16pp section)
pulling	same as 'picking' →
pulp	fibrous material of vegetable origin, from which paper is made; may be produced either by chemical or mechanical means, or combination of both
pulps	derogative term applied to down-market periodicals on pulpy paper
punching shapes	those available for various mechanical binding forms, both loose-leaf and permanent, are:

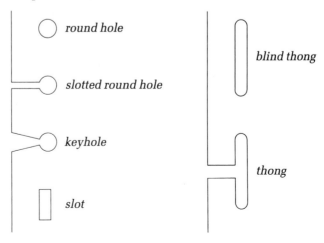

puppet animation	in film animation, manipulating flexible or articulated three-dimensional figures with minute movements and photographing each position by 'stop-frame' →
put down/put up	instruction to printer: change to lower case/change to caps
put to bed	when letterpress formes, lithoplates or gravure plates are secured to presses ready for printing, they are said to be 'put to bed'
PVA	initials of *polyvinyl alcohol*: 'cold melt' → adhesive commonly used in book binding
PVT	initials of '*page view terminal*'
pyramid graph	form of 'coordinate graph' → devised mainly to display specific information about population:

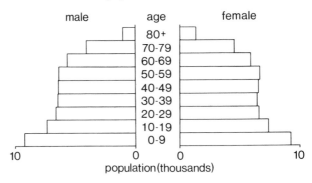

pyramid of vision	configuration present in 'perspective projection' →, formed by visual rays (projectors) from fixed station point extending to corners of picture plane; this concept is basic to 'view volume' → model used in computer graphics

Q

quad	type space, most commonly as 'em-quad' → or 'en-quad' → but also available in widths of 1½, 2, 3 and 4 ems of set
quad centre	setting lines of type so that word spaces are even (that is, not adjusted to make both edges align vertically) and centred for width, giving edges that are both 'ragged' →
quad right/left	same as 'ragged left/right'
quadding	driving abnormal space (eg: en-quads and em-quads) between words in order to fill out line; also used in reference to ranging left and right ('quad left/quad right') and centring ('quad centre') in linecaster composition and photocomposition

quadrilateral	plane figure bounded by four straight lines; there are six types:

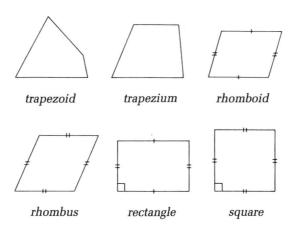

trapezoid   *trapezium*   *rhomboid*

rhombus   *rectangle*   *square*

Quantel Paintbox	trade name for machine developed by Quantel (UK) in early 1980s from their earlier 'DPE' → system; allows hands-on manipulation of moving image by designer, both for broadcast television and video
quarter bound	book having case of which spine is covered in one material and rest in another:

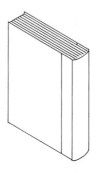

quarto, 4to	cut or folded sheet that is one quarter of basic sheet size
quartz iodine lamp	see 'tungsten halogen lamp'
Qube	name of 'videotex' → network developed by Warner Amex
quire	one twentieth of 'ream' → ; usually 24 or 25 sheets
quirewise stitching	less common name for 'saddle stitch' →
quoin (pron: coyn)	in letterpress, expandable device used to take up space and lock up type 'forme' → ready for press
quotes, quote marks	usually, inverted commas before, and apostrophes after, a word, phrase or passage of text to show that it is quoted

qv (pl: qqv)	abbreviation for *quod vide*, Latin for 'which see'; used in footnotes and glossaries to indicate cross-reference
QWERT/QWERTY keyboard	acronym denoting standard typewriter keyboard layout, derived from order of characters on first alphabetic line (qwertyuiop); also commonly used for photocomposition keyboards

R

®	registered design mark, used to indicate that design has been officially registered, as measure of protection against plagiarism
RA paper sizes	see 'A, B and C Series'
racking-up (computers)	same as 'scrolling' →
radiation drying	use of infra-red or ultra-violet radiation to accelerate drying-time of inks and varnishes
radix	basis of numbering or notation system, involving 'positional notation' →; in decimal notation, radix is 10, in 'binary notation' → it is 2, in 'octal notation' → it is 8, and in 'hexadecimal notation' → it is 16
rag paper	one largely made from rag pulp; used for best quality writings
ragged right/left	setting lines of type so that, though they are all set to standard measure, word spaces are not adjusted to make both edges align vertically (see 'ranged right/left'); also described as 'unjustified on right/left' or 'quad right/left':

Existing on-line systems have made it possible to
obtain bibliographic references in seconds – but have
only partly tackled the problem of obtaining the
original document, a process which can take weeks.

ragged right

Existing on-line systems have made it possible to
obtain bibliographic references in seconds – but have
only partly tackled the problem of obtaining the
original document, a process which can take weeks.

ragged left

raised capital	same as 'cocked-up initial' →

raised point/dot	full point raised from usual position on base line (.) to position halfway up cap height (·) usually as decimal point, eg: 29·5; also known in US as 'centered dot'
RAM (computers)	acronym for *r*andom *a*ccess *m*emory: 'memory' → into which data can be inserted ('written'), as well as being 'read', in comparison with 'ROM' →
Rand tablet (computers)	trade name for the make of 'digitizing pad' →
random access memory	see 'RAM'
random scan (computer graphics)	method of plotting discrete points on VDU screen, then joining them with lines drawn by means of 'vector' → generator; also known as 'vector scan'
random/scatter proof	in lithography, proof of illustration matter (especially in four colour process) arranged in random pattern unrelated to imposition and layout on print job; made to show quality and accuracy of 'halftone process' → work
ranged left/right	if one edge of block of type lines is said to be 'ragged' → or 'unjustified', the other is 'ranged'; more commonly referred to in US as 'align left/right'
ranging figures	same as 'lining figures' → but less suitable term
raster (computer graphics)	German for 'screen', whether of ruled transparent plate used in halftone process or of scan pattern on surface of 'CRT' →; hence, by extension, surface itself
raster scan (computer graphics)	tracing on screen of cathode ray tube by electronic beam of rapid succession of parallel lines, coded to delineate digital or analog images, as compared to 'random scan' → or 'vector mode' →:

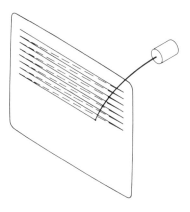

| **raster scan display processing unit** (computers) | one incorporating image-creation system, refresh buffer (also known as 'bit map'), image refresh system, CRT display and interaction device: |

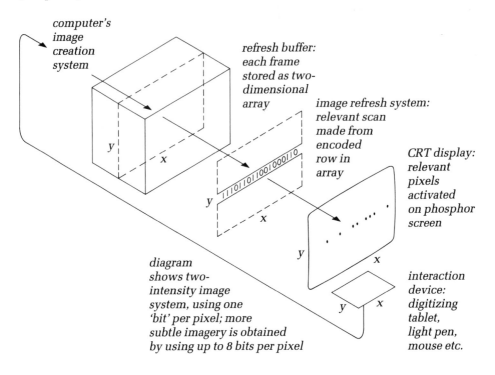

computer's image creation system

refresh buffer: each frame stored as two-dimensional array

image refresh system: relevant scan made from encoded row in array

CRT display: relevant pixels activated on phosphor screen

diagram shows two-intensity image system, using one 'bit' per pixel; more subtle imagery is obtained by using up to 8 bits per pixel

interaction device: digitizing tablet, light pen, mouse etc.

raw data	1) data intended for output that has not undergone some processing for machine 'reading', which may or may not be necessary; 2) data output that has not been edited to remove characters relating only to machine-processing functions
raw tape	same as 'unjustified tape' → and 'idiot tape'
RC paper	abbreviation for 'resin-coated paper' →
reaction shot	in cinefilm and TV, 'cutaway' → to show reaction of one of film characters to main action
read-only memory (computers)	see 'ROM'
read/write head (computers)	electronmagnet designed to extract signals from, or implant them into, magnetic disk, tape or drum
reader	see 'copyreader', 'printer's reader' and 'publisher's reader'
reader-printer	machine for reading 'microform' → information and making print-out enlargements

readout (computers)   output via VDU, also known as 'soft copy'

real time processing (computers)   system involving use of 'interactive display' →, 'interrogating typewriter' → or indeed any input device that can communicate with machine without delay and receive immediate response, eg: airline booking system

ream   standard quantity of paper containing 472, 480, 500, 504 or 516 sheets, according to nature of material; but note that in Europe, paper is now standardized in units of 1,000 (mille)

rear projection   same as 'back projection' →

rebus   representation of certain words in sentence by pictures, typically to form child's puzzle:

record (computers)   item of information entered on 'file' → in form suited to nature of file store, eg: magnetic tape

recto   any right-hand page of book; one that is odd-numbered

redundancy   in communication studies, way in which messages are reinforced by repetition and syntax to avoid misunderstanding by recipient:

to the zoo ▶

this way to the zoo ▶

reel-fed   same as 'web-fed' →

re-etch   submitting letterpress or gravure plate to additional etching so as to modify printed image

reference marks   those type characters that key footnotes to text above, usually appearing in following order:

| asterisk | dagger | double dagger | section | parallel | paragraph |

reflection copy   opaque matter for reproduction that is photographed by reflected light in processing, as against transparent subject matter that is photographed by back-lighting

reformatting
(photocomposition)   establishing new parameters for typesetting of copy already proofed or printed

refresh display
(computer graphics)   'CRT' → display requiring systematic refreshing of light output of phosphor owing to automatic decay (normally within 50 microseconds)

refresh rate
(computer graphics)   rate at which 'CRT' → display is refreshed, typically 30–60 cycles per second for 'raster scan' → display

region filling
(computer graphics)   in VDU display graphics, implementation of interactive program routine that fills in area or region on screen defined by boundary with 'pixels' → of appropriate colour or tone:

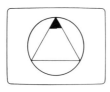 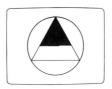 

register   two or more print impressions in their correct relationship on sheet; hence 'in register' and 'out of register'

register marks   marks on a printed sheet appearing outside area of job when trimmed to size, used to ensure accurate register

registered design   one that has been accepted as such by UK Patent Office, 'design' in this case being defined as 'features of shape, configuration, pattern or ornament applied to an article by any industrial process or means'

reglet   another name for 'clump' →, especially one made of wood

regular polygon   plane figure having equal angles and equal sides; some regular polygons are:

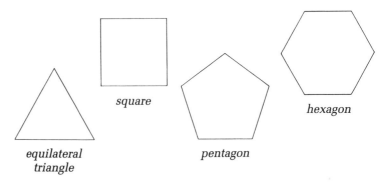

equilateral triangle   square   pentagon   hexagon

regular solid	one bounded by plane surfaces that are 'regular polygons' →; there are five regular convex solids:

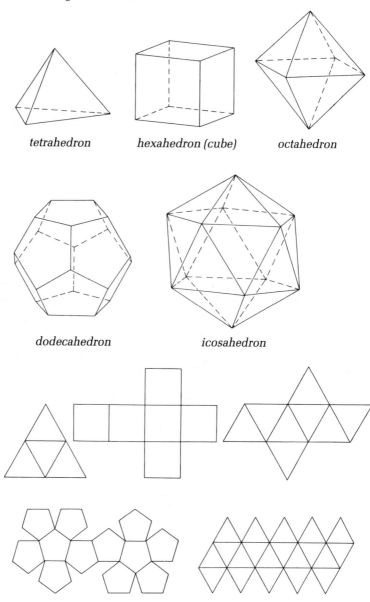

tetrahedron *hexahedron (cube)* *octahedron*

dodecahedron *icosahedron*

opened-out patterns of regular solids

release paper	backing material for peel-off print or stationery items
release print	in cinefilm, final print intended for showing to audience; also known as 'showprint'

relief printing	general term for those printing processes in which inked image is on raised surface, as in 'letterpress' → or 'flexography' →
relief stamping	same as 'die-stamping' →
remainders	copies of book that is no longer selling at its original published price, reduced to clear stock; fate worse than death for any author
remote access (computers)	technique of accessing computer direct from distant terminal over communication lines
repaint (computer graphics)	recompose or modify graphic display on screen
reprint	make subsequent printing (impression) of publication; reprints of single features or distinct portions of publication are known as 'separates' → or 'offprints' → (though these may also be part of first impression)
repro, repro proof	proof from type matter, made with great care on special proofing press using best quality coated paper, for use in photomechanical reproduction
reprographic printing	general term to cover work done by spirit duplicating, ink duplicating, electrostatic printing and small offset printing
reprotyping	typing intended for photomechanical reproduction
rescreen	'halftone process' → applied to subject matter that has already been screened, either by 'dot-for-dot' → or by careful angling of halftone screen to avoid 'screen clash' →
resin-coated paper	photographic material in which sensitized paper is sandwiched between polyethylene layers; also known as 'PE' or 'RC' paper
resist	chemical applied to printing plate to stop or reduce etching process
resolution	in photography and photomechanical reproduction ability of lens, film or mirror system to allow fine detail to be produced and read; sometimes expressed in terms of lines per centimetre
resolution (computer graphics)	measure of density of scanned observations, known as 'picture elements' → or 'pixels' in any graphic display, calculated in observations per square inch (see also 'high resolution scanning')
response frame (computers)	VDU 'frame' → requesting or implying reply from user
response time	time taken for machine, such as computer, to respond to user command
retainer fee	sum of money exacted annually by consultant designer from client for doing nothing in particular

reticulation	in photography, wrinkling and crazing of emulsion of film, causing grain to cluster in visible blobs
retouching	skilled alteration of halftone originals to improve or correct, using 'airbrush' →, brush, pencil, scalpel or dyes
retree	name for substandard batch of paper
reversal film	normal form of colour film, in which image is positive and can be projected as slide; also, special purpose contact film in which tone values of original are kept
reverse b to w	instruction to printer: reverse image from black to white
reverse field VDT	terminal that can display dark images on light background as alternative; also known as 'reverse contrast'
reverse indent	see 'hanging indent'
reverse l to r	instruction to printer: reverse image from left to right
reverse leading	see 'reverse line-feed'
reverse line-feed	in photocomposition, facility for turning film or paper back to previously set line so as to make additions, useful in tabular setting; also known as 'negative line-feed' (unsuitable because of ambiguity about 'negative') and 'reverse leading' (unsuitable because of reference to hot-metal setting)
reverse out	same as 'save out' →
reverse out type	in photomechanical reproduction, instruction to 'save out' type image from background
reverse P	colloquialism for 'paragraph mark' →
reverse-reading	reading right to left, as on letterpress printing surface or on some photocomposition film output; also known as 'wrong-reading'
reverse scrolling (computer graphics)	as 'scrolling' → but with lines of text moving down instead of up, so as to review previously displayed lines
reverse video	in CRT display, alphanumeric and other graphic signs shown dark on light background in place of customary light display on dark background
revise (proof)	additional proof to show that corrections from earlier proof have been properly made
RF	in cartography, initials of 'representative fraction', used to denote scale relationship between distance shown on map and actual distance on ground, eg: 1/50,000

RGB colour cube (computer graphics)	model for colour specification that forms basis for video colour coding:

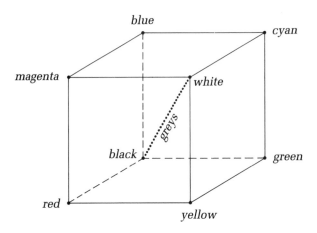

RGB colour system	one based on additive primaries red/green/blue, in contrast to 'CMY colour system' →; see also 'additive colour mixing'
RH	initials of 'relative humidity': important aspect of environmental control in print shop since it affects behaviour of paper, which may stretch or shrink during printing with humidity changes
rhp	initials of 'right-hand page'
riga tipografica	Italian 12pt typographical unit of measurement, identical to 'cicero' → in France and Germany; called 'riga' for short
right-angle fold	folding a piece of paper in half, then in half again at right angle; standard fold for book sections (see 'folding methods')
right-handed coordinates (computer graphics)	'coordinate graph' → system involving depth dimension, denoted by 'z' coordinate extending in this fashion:

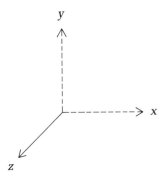

188

right-reading   reading left to right, as on offset lithography printing plate

rigid disk   same as 'hard disk' →
(computers)

ring binder   see 'binding methods'

RIP   initials of 'rest in proportion'; instruction to indicate that all elements are to be reduced or enlarged in same proportion

RIP   initials of 'raster image processor' →
(computer graphics)

rising front   device on some cameras whereby lens can be adjusted in relation to film so that 'converging verticals' → can be corrected:

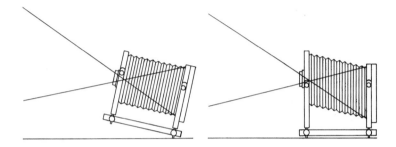

river (of type)   undesirable white streak straggling down through lines of type, caused by coalescing word spaces, sometimes known as 'window'

roller caption   in cinefilm and TV, titles and credits to movie or feature, set out on roll of black paper that is wound through aperture on machine and shot by camera:

rolling ball	attachment to VDU that permits operator to change or adapt images
(computers)	on screen:

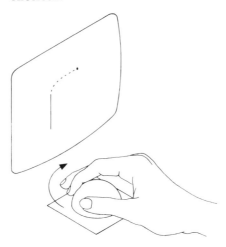

rom	abbreviation used in proof correction to show that word of passage should be reset in upright (*rom*an) type
ROM (computers)	acronym for 'read-*o*nly *m*emory': that part of computer's data store containing permanent contents such as application programs and system programs that can only be 'read' →, not altered, augmented or erased, as against 'RAM' → (but see also 'PROM' and 'EPROM')
roman	very general term to cover all typefaces deriving from humanistic manuscripts, as distinct from black letter (gothic); also used to distinguish non-italic and non-bold letterforms
roman numerals	before introduction of arabic numerals, roman numbers were the norm, but are now only used for chapter headings, lists and dates; capital letters are used, in the following manner:

I	II	III	IV	V	VI	VII	VIII	IX	X
one	two	three	four	five	six	seven	eight	nine	ten

L	C	D	M
fifty	one hundred	five hundred	one thousand

convention whereby I before V (5–1) = 4 and I before X = 9 is also carried on to higher values, XL = 40, XC = 90, CD = 400, CM = 900, MXM = 1990

ROP	1) initials of 'run-*o*f-*p*ress'; instruction to printer to run off all paper available for particular job, regardless of job order 2) in newspapers, colour work printed with body of paper ('run-of-paper'), as against pre-printed colour
rose diagram	see 'star graph'

rostrum
(film animation)

camera mount with movable carriage for camera and movable tabletop for artwork beneath it; also known as 'animation stand':

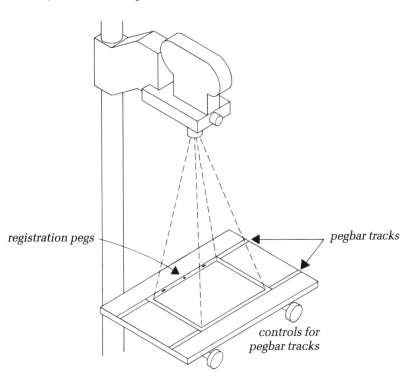

registration pegs

pegbar tracks

controls for
pegbar tracks

rotary press

machine in which printing surface is cylindrical; may be either 'sheet-fed' or 'web-fed' →:

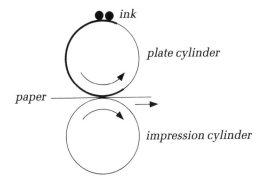

ink

plate cylinder

paper

impression cylinder

rotogravure

photogravure printing on web-fed rotary press

rough

sketch design for printed material, not always as 'rough' as term implies; there is even, ludicrous as it may seem, a 'finished rough'

round 'and'

same as 'ampersand' →

191

rounding and backing

shaping book after sewing so that back is convex and foredge concave and to provide an edge on which to secure cover boards:

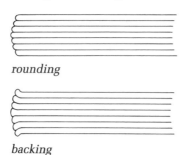

rounding

backing

routine (computers)

part of computer program relating to special function, hence input routine, error routine, output routine and so on

routing

in letterpress, physical removal of material in those parts of printing plate that are not to print

row

in tabular or 'matrix' → display, horizontal line of characters or symbols (vertical line being 'column')

RS-232-C

standard established by US Electronic Industries Association relating to data transfer between computer systems

rubber-banding (computer graphics)

in computer graphics, manipulation of 'stylus' → or 'cursor' → to construct drawing by stretching line from fixed point:

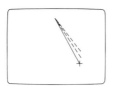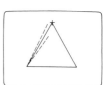

Rubin's vase/face figure

image devised by E Rubin in 1915 and used by perceptual psychologists and others to demonstrate visual ambiguity arising from figure/ground confusion:

rubric

heading of book chapter or section, printed in red to contrast with text in black

ruling pen	precision drawing instrument suitable for fine artwork:

ruling-up table	same as 'lining-up table' →
run	see 'print run'
run (computers)	execution of one 'program' → or 'routine' →
run in	US term instructing typesetter to set two paragraphs as one (equivalent to 'run on' in UK)
run-length encoding (computers)	technique devised to speed up input of image-building instructions by handling 'picture elements' → in groups of like value
run-of-paper	in periodical and newspaper publishing, any placing of advertisement which is not especially advantageous (see also 'preferred position')
run on	1) proof correction or manuscript alteration: 'do not start new line or paragraph' (US: run in) 2) item often listed in print quotations, giving price for increasing print quantity by specified amount
run out	'photoprint' or film output from photocomposition machine
run-through work	use of special ruling machine to print parallel lines across sheet from one edge to other without breaks; see also 'feint lines'
runability	fearsome expression intended to describe suitability of paper or board for machine-handling processes other than that encompassed by 'printability' → or breakability and stretchability of paper
runaround	typesetting in which lines of type are set to fit round an illustration or other display matter
runners	marginal numbers placed at regular intervals to give quick reference for text lines, especially of poetry
running foot	type line below main text, giving book title and/or chapter title
running head(line)	type line above main text, giving book title and/or chapter title
running text	continuous text matter, arranged in columns, as against tabular or displayed matter

S

Sabattier effect (photography) one in which partly developed photographic print is given second exposure, resulting in partial reversal of tones; also referred to as 'solarization' →

saccadic movement brief, rapid eye movement from one fixed point to another, as when reading

saddle-stitch, saddle-wire to secure book by means of thread or wire through back fold of insetted work; though 'saddle-stitch' is often used for wire as well as thread, this is not recommended because of possible confusion

saddleback book one having 'insetted work' which is secured through back fold by wire or thread stitches

safe area in TV, that central portion of transmitted picture which can be guaranteed to remain visible on ordinary domestic receiver

safelight in photography, coloured lamp used in darkrooms when developing or printing sensitized materials

same-size (abb: s/s) instruction to printer to make print image same size as original

sampling (computer graphics) making test series of observations of signal values at specific intervals

sans serif, sanserif type face not having finishing strokes at ends of character elements:

ABC abc

Sanson-Flamsteed's equal-area projection global projection in which equator is twice length of central meridian and poles are pointed, as distinct from 'Mollweide's projection' →; projection is much improved by interrupting it through oceans:

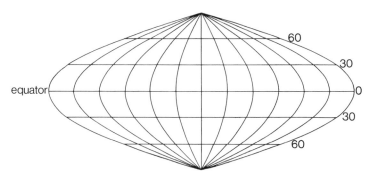

Sanson-Flamsteed's equal area

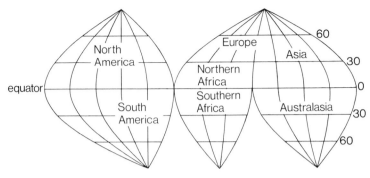

Sanson-Flamsteed's interrupted

save (computers)   colloquial synonym for instruction to 'store' → data

save out   in photomechanical reproduction, to produce white lettering or line image on solid or halftone ground; also referred to, especially in US, as 'drop out'

SC paper   abbreviation for 'supercalendered paper' →

sc, s caps   abbreviations for 'small caps' →

scaling, scaling-up   working out degree of enlargement or reduction of original for reproduction, so that this can be shown by dimension and percentage marks on overlay; arrived at by means of 'diagonal' method or 'proportional scale' method:

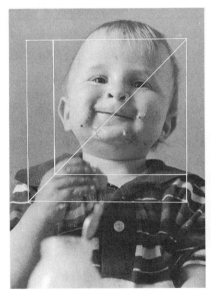
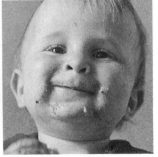

larger white rectangle in illustration on left is actual size required; this is contracted as diagonal to form smaller rectangle; final image is on right

195

scamp used in advertising to describe quick sketch not intended to show more than general idea

scan conversion transforming data-stored images into an array of 'picture elements'
(computer graphics) →, or 'vector' → images into 'raster' → images

scanner electronic machine that derives digital data from scan of opaque or transparent subject matter, now primarily by means of laser illumination, and transfers them to output device that converts them to film 'scaled' → and screened ready for print reproduction

scatter graph one representing separate values which may not be connected as line graph and which give only general trend of relationship:

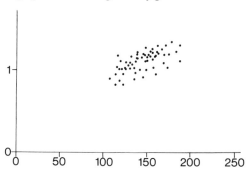

scatter proofs in photomechanical processing, proofs of illustrations in random pattern unrelated to layout

scatter/random proof in lithography, proof of illustration matter (especially in four colour process) arranged in random pattern unrelated to imposition and layout on print job; made to show quality and accuracy of 'halftone process' → work

schema synopsis or outline, especially one in diagram form

Schuster's fork impossible figure devised by Schuster in 1964; also known as 'Devil's tuning fork':

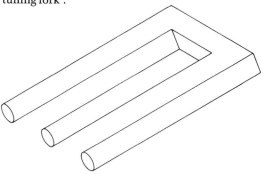

score same as 'crease' →

scraperboard	drawing material with heavy coating of china clay which can be scraped after covering with black ink to give an effect of 'white-line' engraving also known, especially in US, as 'scratchboard'
scratch comma	punctuation mark in form of oblique stroke
screamer	slang for exclamation mark
screen angle	angle at which halftone screen is arranged; whenever two or more halftones are to overprint, to avoid screen clash:

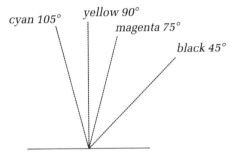

four colour printing

screen clash	undesirable pattern resulting from overprinting of two or more halftones at unsuitable screen angles (see also 'moiré'):

screen cursor (computers)	see 'cursor'
screen finder	same as 'screen tester' →
screen, halftone	see 'halftone process'

197

screen mode
(computer graphics)

in word-processing and photocomposition, text display format on VDU, available most commonly in single-column mode, dual-column mode or split-screen mode:

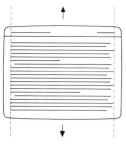 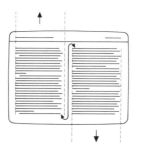 

*single column
(sequential)*

*dual column (sequential,
second column containing
continuation of same text)*

*split-screen (not
sequential, used for
merging two texts or for
updating) each half
of screen is independent*

**screen (process)
printing**

one in which squeegee forces ink through fine screen of fabric or metal to which is fixed a stencil:

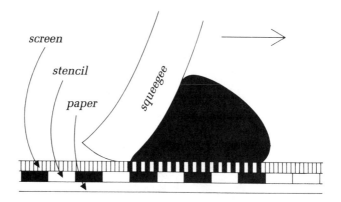

photographic, rather than cut, stencils are now common, and high speed, high quality screen printing is now possible

screen tester

device which, if laid on printed halftone and rotated until symmetrical moiré pattern → is produced, will indicate screen size

**screened positive/
negative**

film, whether monochrome or as 'colour separations' → converted into reproducible form by use of 'halftone screen' →, suitable for 'printing-down' → on plate

screenless photolitho

process using troughs or peaks of grained aluminium plate as image receptors in positive or negative workings respectively, instead of photomechanical halftone screen

screenload (VDU)   maximum number of characters than can appear in one 'frame' →

script (type)   typeface designed in imitation of writing done with pen or brush, often having characters made to fit closely as in joined writing:

$$\mathscr{AB\ Cabcde}$$

scrolling
(computer graphics)   in VDU display, form of presentation in which, as last available line of screen is filled with characters, top line is deleted and all lines are moved up so that new line can be entered at bottom; also known as 'racking-up':

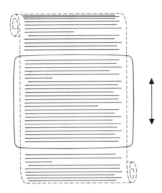

scumming   in lithography, fault in which water-accepting layer is worn away from non-image areas, giving dirty-looking impression

search (computers)   essential facility built into machine that enables it to hunt for information within its data store, or those of on-line 'databases' →, by means of key words, phrases or codes

search and replace
(computers)   procedure relating to correction, editing and 'protocol conversion' → whereby specified words or codes are searched for and amended as required

SECAM   acronym for *Se*quentiale *C*ouleur *à M*émoire: 625-line colour television broadcasting standard developed in France and adopted in other countries, including USSR

secondary colour   one resulting from combination of two 'primary colours' →

section   sheet of paper folded into four or more pages to make into gathered or insetted book; also known as 'signature', especially in US

section mark   type character indicating beginning of new section; also used as fourth order of 'reference marks' → for footnotes

section-sewn book	one in which gathered sections are secured by sewn thread (see 'binding methods')
sector (computers)	smallest unit of memory on 'magnetic disk' → or 'magnetic drum' → that may be separately located or addressed
sector chart	same as 'pie chart' →
see-through	degree to which image on underlying surface can be seen through sheet of paper
seed filling (computer graphics)	form of 'region filling' → in which one 'pixel' → given correct value will pass on this value to all others within boundary of region
segmented bar graph	see 'bar graph/chart'
selective focusing	in photography, using lens at full, or near full, aperture to focus on particular subject throwing background and/or foreground out-of-focus:

focused at 60cm, f4 aperture   *focused at 120cm, f4 aperture*

Selectric	trade name for popular make of direct impression, or 'strike-on', composing machine
self-cover	book cover made of same material as leaves of book
self-ends	'endpapers' → which are part of first and last sections of book
self-mailer	promotion piece that is sent through post without separate envelope
semantics	see 'semiotic(s)'
semaphore code	one devised for signalling by movements of arms, human or mechanical:

200

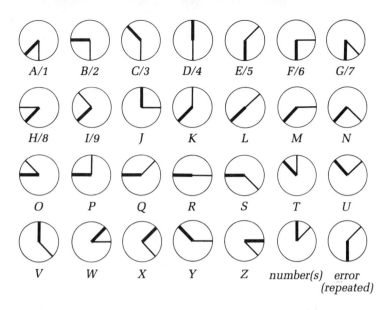

thick stroke = right arm

A/1 · B/2 · C/3 · D/4 · E/5 · F/6 · G/7

H/8 · I/9 · J · K · L · M · N

O · P · Q · R · S · T · U

V · W · X · Y · Z · number(s) · error (repeated)

semiconductor
(electronics)

material whose conductivity varies according to temperature (see 'silicon chip')

semiotic(s), semiology

study of nature and use of signs, whether spoken, gesticulated, written, printed or constructed; divided into three levels, syntactics (relations between signs), semantics (relations between signs and things they refer to) and pragmatics (relations between signs and those who use them):

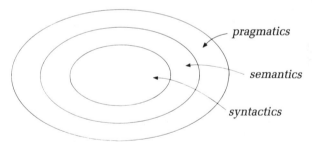

pragmatics

semantics

syntactics

separate (as noun)

same as 'offprint' →

separation artwork

separate drawings for each colour of a colour illustration, usually by means of opaque base artwork and transparent overlays keyed together by 'register marks' →

sepia toning

in photography, treating bromide prints with special chemicals (toners) to produce brown image

serif

finishing strokes or terminals at ends of type characters

serigraphy

another name for 'silk-screen process' →

201

servo mechanism, servo	device whose function is to control operation of machine by detecting and minimizing difference between its intended and its actual performance
set (of metal type)	measure of relative width of type character; in Monotype machine composition, all characters (including spaces) have 'set' width, expressed in units, which are not standard dimensions, like points, but are related to proportion of typeface design; widest character is divided into 18 equal units, other characters are allocated unit values in proportion:

set (photocomposition)	measure of relative width of type character; varies according to individual system and to spacing adjustments provided within system itself, resulting in specifiers' nightmare
set and hold	instruction to printer to set an item and hold it for future use, as, for example, an obituary
set-off	still-wet impression making mark on adjacent sheet just after printing; sometimes (confusingly) called 'offset'
set-off spray	attachment to printing machine that sprays fine powder on each sheet as it comes off press, so as to avoid 'set-off' →
set solid	type set without 'leading' → or other additional interlinear spacing
set-square	triangular drawing implement made of transparent plastic
set theory	mathematical theory concerning description and operation of sets, ie: collections of items having at least one property in common; symbols used in set mathematics are:

{....}	*set*	$\subset$	*is a proper subset of*
$\in$	*is a member of*	$\subseteq$	*is a subset of*
$\notin$	*is not a member of*	$\cup$	*set union*
ϕ		$\cap$	*set intersection*
Φ	*the empty set, or the null set*	$\mathscr{E}$	*universal set sometimes shown as U or μ*
{ }			
$=$	*is equal to*	$'$	*complement*
$\neq$	*is not equal to*	$n(\ )$	*number of set*

set-up key	in film animation, instruction given to camera operator on camera movements and 'field sizes' →
sewn book	any book secured with sewn thread
sexto, 6to	cut or folded sheet which is one sixth of basic sheet size
SG (of paper)	initials of 'short *grain*' →
SGML	initials of *S*tandard *G*eneralized *M*ark-up *L*anguage, devised to convert word-processor output for use on photocomposition machines
shade (of colour)	result of admixing small amounts of black with basic hue
shaded letter	'outline letter' → with shadow effect running down one side of strokes, thus:

SPECIMEN

shank (of type)	main part of piece of type by which it is raised to printing height (see 'type')
shear (of type)	angle at which character stroke is terminated:

Ee

sheet	whole piece of paper, flat or folded; there are many basic sheet sizes in printing (see 'paper sizes')
sheet-fed	printing machine in which paper is fed one sheet at a time as distinct from 'reel- / web-fed' →
sheet proof	one taken from a forme; also called an 'imposed proof'
sheet stock	printed sheets held in store for binding up
sheet work	form of imposition in which pages on one side of sheet are in one forme and those for other side are in another forme; see also 'half-sheet work'
sheeter	machine that cuts reel (web) of paper into sheets of prescribed length
sheetwise	most common printing method, in which sheet is printed first on one side, then on the other, to produce complete section as distinct from 'half-sheet work' →

shift key	in keyboard, one that, when depressed, converts set of keys to another mode; typically from lower case to capitals
shilling mark	old name for 'solidus' →, 'oblique stroke', 'slash' or 'virgule'
short and	same as 'ampersand' →
short grain (of paper)	indication in specification or quotation for print that shorter dimensions of sheet runs with grain of paper (see 'grain direction')
short ink	one that tends to be crumbly and cannot be rolled into thin film
shoulder (of type)	non-printing area surrounding face of type, and from which it rises (see 'type')
shoulder note	one that is set in side margin at head of paragraph
show-through	degree to which image on reverse of sheet shows through paper
showprint	same as 'release print' →
shriek	slang for 'exclamation mark'
shutter, between-the-lens	camera shutter that opens by means of pivoting, interleaved blades
shutter, focal plane	camera shutter, consisting of two blinds on either side of narrow slit, travelling across film on rollers; slit varies in width according to exposure time
SI unit	metric unit of measure conforming to *Système Internationale*
SIAD	initials of *Society of Industrial Artists and Designers* (UK), founded in 1930; well-meaning but somewhat ineffectual affair which has neither exclusivity of professional body like Law Society nor bargaining power of trade union (now renamed Chartered Society of Designers)
sic	Latin for 'thus', used within parentheses to confirm accuracy of preceding word, usually because of unorthodox spelling
side-heading	heading in side margin at top of page or paragraph
side note	short portion of text matter positioned in margin of page
side stab/stitch	to secure book by means of wire forced through side close to back
SIGGRAPH	acronym for *Special Interest Group on* (computer) *Graphics*, sponsored by Association for Computing Machinery (US)
sign	in communication studies, any means whereby one human, animal or plant seeks to affect behaviour or condition of another by communication; 'sign-types' are those universals (such as letters of

alphabet) which are drawn on to produce 'sign-events', physical embodiment of sign-types (such as speech or piece of writing)

sign on, sign off
(computers)

same as 'logon' →, 'logoff' →

signature

letter or number printed at bottom of first page of each section of book, to ensure correct sequence; also (especially in US), synonym for 'section' →

silhouette halftone

one in which the outline follows the shape of some part of subject of illustration (same as 'cut-out')

silicon chip

tiny sliver (typically about 6mm square) of semi-conductor element silicon, containing set of 'integrated circuits' →; in form of 'micro-processor' → silicon chips form central processing unit of micro-computer (and, increasingly, of all computers), though they are likely to be upstaged by even more compact 'bubble memory' → devices

silkscreen process

traditional form of 'screen process' → in which screen is made of silk, still used for fine art prints; also known as 'serigraphy'

single-lens reflex

see 'camera types'

sixteen-mo, 16mo

cut or folded sheet that is one sixteenth of basic sheet size

sixteen-sheet

poster size of 120×80in (305×203cm)

size

chemical incorporated in 'furnish' → of paper to hold cellulose fibres together and bind them to any coating that may be applied

sketching
(computer graphics)

facility in some graphics displays whereby sketches may be drawn on screen

sketchpad
(computer graphics)

first real-time interactive computer graphics system, involving use of 'light pen' → as drawing tool; devised in US by Ivan Sutherland in 1962

skew

align incorrectly, as on VDU display, hard copy printout or facsimile transmission

skew character

one in set of 'OCR' → set that is unreadable due to misalignment

skew failure

machine-readable document rendered unreadable due to poor alignment

skip

in photogravure printing, missing dots resulting from poor inking

skip-framing

in cinefilm, deleting given number of film frames from shot at regular intervals, to reduce running time or speed up action

skyline
(of newspaper)

banner headline running above nameplate

slab-serif	typeface with markedly square-ended serifs which may or may not be 'bracketed' →:

ABCDEFGHIJKLMN
The bank recognize

slash	same as 'oblique stroke', 'virgule' and 'solidus' →; more common in US
slave unit (computers)	any device without its own central processing unit which depends entirely for its working on control from 'main-frame' → system
slide binder	see 'plastic grip/slide spine'
slip	long, narrow strip of paper used for 'galley proof' →
slip case	container for book or set of books, made so that spine is left visible:

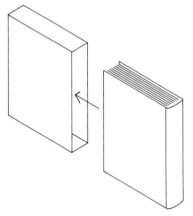

slip page	proof made up on 'slip' → but separated out as → pages
slip proof	same as 'galley proof' → but may also be taken to mean 'slip page'
slip-sheeting	US term for 'interleaving' →
sloped roman	correct term for many typefaces which are generally known as italics even though they are not 'cursive' →; see 'italic' for illustration
SLR	initials of 'single lens reflex' (see 'camera types')
slug	line of hot-metal type cast as continuous piece on line composing machine; also, in US, slab of less-than-type-high material, known in UK as 'clump'
slur	fault in printing caused by movement during making of impression

slurred dot (type)	termination of certain characters, resembling distorted dot:

k

small caps (abbr: sc, s caps)	smaller version of capital letters, about same height as 'x-height' → of lower case letters
small face	smaller of two sizes available on same body of metal type
snoot	in photographic lighting, cone-shaped device fitted in front of spotlight to give very narrow light beam:

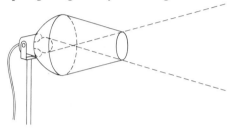

soft paper	in photography, one giving low contrast image
soft copy (computers)	output displayed on electronic screen, as contrasted with 'hard copy' →
soft copy keyboard (computers)	one producing image of text on electronic screen but not, in first instance, in permanent form on paper or film
soft cover	one not made from stiff board
soft dot	in 'halftone process' →, one that shades off at its edges
soft keyboard (computers)	VDU display resembling keyboard, characters or symbols of which are activated by 'light pen' →; as distinct from 'soft copy keyboard' →
soft typesetter (computers)	input device that generates typesetting and displays it on screen, but does not allow editing
software (computers)	'programs' → of computer, as against 'hardware' →
software house (computers)	company specializing in writing software for its clients
solarization (photography)	accidental over-exposure of photographic negative or print resulting in partial reversal of tones; often used (incorrectly) as synonym for 'Sabattier effect' →
solid modelling (computer graphics)	realistic on-screen representation of 3D objects

207

solidus	oblique stroke, thus: /; used to denote alternatives, ratios and fractions; also called 'slash', 'oblique' or 'virgule' (though this, confusingly, is understood by some to mean 'comma')
solus position	advertisement space on page where there is no other advertisement
SOM (computers)	initials of 'start-of-message'
sort	single piece of type; a 'special sort' is one not usually included in fount, but available on order
SP	initials of 'station point' →
space	type matter which does not print, used to separate words (see 'word-spacing')
spaceband	wedge device used in mechanical type composition to provide variable word spacing
spec (pron: speck or spess)	slang for 'specification': definition of data and procedures required to execute task
special sort	type character not normally included in 'font/fount' →
specimen page	one set up and proofed to show effect of proposed layout style
specular reflexion	effect observed on any shining surface, eg: highlight on polished sphere
speed-rating (of film)	see 'film speed'
spelling checker	part of word-processor or photocomposition program that recognizes misspellings in input and marks them for correction
spine	that edge of book at which leaves and covers are secured; also called 'back' and 'backbone' (see 'book')
spiral binder	one in which leaves are secured by spiral wire wound through small, pre-drilled holes; sometimes, but totally inaccurately, applied to plastic comb binder (see 'binding methods'):

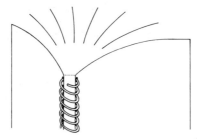

spirit duplicating	simple planographic printing process for up to 100 copies by means

of aniline dye transfer printing onto plain sheets moistened with spirit solvent

splayed 'M'   one like this:

M

splicer   in cinefilm, mechanical device used to hold two pieces of film in proper position for splicing by means of tape, cement or hot-splice

split dash/rule   one like these:

split duct/fountain   device to divide ink supply so that two or three colours may be printed at once on same sheet; also used to obtain blending of colours

split fraction   same as 'piece fraction' →

split-screen mode (VDU)   see 'screen mode'

spoils, spoilage   sheets that are badly printed and so not included in delivered quantity of job; printers usually allow for this by printing 'overs' (US term: makeovers)

spot size (computer graphics)   in 'vector display' →, diameter of spot focused on 'phosphor' → of screen, hence thickness of line created by extension of spot

spotmeter   in photography, light meter with very limited angle of view, such as are incorporated in many reflex cameras; measures light value only of that portion of scene central to view

spotting   delicate form of photo-retouching, solely concerned with eliminating small processing blemishes from prints; almost always an essential finishing task when making first quality prints

spraygun   same as 'airbrush' →

spread   pair of facing pages, left-hand and right-hand; often considered as design unit even though pages may be printed in different sections; see 'centre spread' and 'fake double'

sprinkled edges   edges of book brushed with colour for decorative effect

209

spur (of type)	short projection on character, especially at base of G:

G
↖ *spur*

square-back book	one in which wrapped, drawn-on or cased cover forms flat spine that is not 'rounded and backed' →
square-serif	same as 'slab-serif' →
squared-up (halftone)	normal form of halftone, in which edges are straight and rectangular
squares (of book)	bookbinders' term for overhanging edges of 'cased book' →
squealer	slang for exclamation mark
SRA paper sizes	see 'A, B and C Series'
SRDS	initials of *S*tandard *R*ate & *D*ata *S*ervice: organization giving details of advertising rates, dimensions and deadlines for US newspapers and periodicals
S/S, s/s	abbreviation for '*same size*' →
stab	same as 'stitch' →
staircase effect (computer graphics)	another name for 'aliasing' → or 'jaggies'
stamping	US term for 'blocking' →
stand-alone	electronic unit to which input must be supplied from outside, as distinct from one linked directly to central computer or operator
stand-alone system (computers)	one that functions without need of connexion to anything other than power supply, having its own 'central processing unit' →
stand camera	see 'camera types'
standard aspect ratio	see 'aspect ratio'
standing time	UK term for time during print production cycle when nothing is happening (US term is 'open time')
standing type/matter	composed type matter kept for possible reprint rather than being melted down or 'dissed'
star graph	one in which values are plotted as radii from point of origin; also known as 'rose diagram' and 'vector diagram':

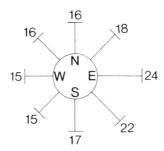

starburst filter   in photography, attachment to camera lens which produces 'star-burst' effect from point source of strong light

stat   abbreviation for 'photostat' →

station point
(abbr: SP)   in 'perspective projections' →, imagined position of eye of observer viewing object

status word
(computers)   indication from computer as to what next action of operator should be, or which gives some kind of warning

STD   initials of 'Society of Typographic Designers' (UK)

stem   main vertical, or near vertical, part of type character

stencil duplication   reproduction process in which ink is forced through stencil of original image onto absorbent paper; often known as 'mimeography' from trade name of best known printing machine in this field

step-and-repeat   photomechanical method of producing multiple images from one original by means of special step-and-repeat machine

step index   one in which steps are cut out of foredge for greater ease of reference; sometimes called 'cut-in' index:

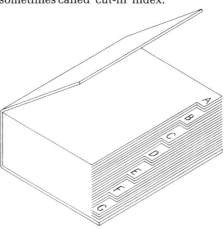

stereo-   prefix meaning 'solid'

211

stereopsis	effect of normal binocular vision in providing depth cues
stereotype, stereo	duplicate letterpress plate cast from mould
stet	Latin for 'let it stand': instruction to leave some part of proof as it was before previous correction was made, though superseded in UK (see 'proof corrections')
stiff-leaves	endpapers → which are glued to whole of first and last leaves in book, rather than just being 'tipped-on' →
still-frame	in use of videotape recorder (VTR), repetitive playback of one picture, equivalent to 'freeze-frame' or 'stop-frame' in cinefilm
still video	transmission, usually by means of telephone network and 'modem' → of static display, whether of photograph, drawing or diagram
stitch	to secure book by forcing wires through back of 'insetted' → work or side of 'gathered' → work
stock	any material to be used for printing on
stone	surface (once made of stone) on which letterpress 'formes' → are imposed before being transferred to bed of press
stone hand	in letterpress printing, one who arranges and secures composed type matter and plates in correct order for printing
stop bath	in photography, diluted acid solution used to arrest development before fixing
stop-cylinder press	'cylinder press' → in which cylinder remains stationary whilst printing bed is returned after being moved out of contact for inking, as distinct from 'two-revolution press' →
stop-frame	operating mode in cinefilm whereby each frame is exposed separately; used in film animation
stop-motion	same as 'freeze-frame' →
storage tube (computer graphics)	VDU display that does not need refreshing (see 'refresh display'); images of this type cannot be modified on-screen
store (computers)	part of machine that houses data and/or program instructions; there are two types, 'main memory' → and 'backing store' →
storyboard	set of preliminary sketches showing how cinefilm or TV sequence is intended to develop and give idea of timing and content without going into detail
straight matter	copy that is marked up for typesetting to standard measure throughout

strap	subsidiary headline placed over main headline of newspaper or periodical feature
strawboard	one made from straw pulp; used for making covers of cased books
stress (type)	direction implied by position of thickest part of rounded characters
stretch-printing	in cinefilm, printing every other film frame twice, especially in order to convert film shot at one speed for projection in another
strike-on composition	same as 'direct impression' →
strike-through	penetration of printing ink through sheet from one side to other
striker	slang for exclamation mark
string (computers)	set of consecutive characters in data store (memory) of computer
stripping in	inserting new or corrected item on 'film assembly' →
stripping up as one	as above, but superimposing them to produce single new image; also known, especially in US, as 'surprinting' or 'double-burning'
stripping up together	combining two or more negatives or positives for photomechanical reproduction
stroke display (computer graphics)	synonym for 'vector display' →
studio camera	see 'camera types'
stuffer	promotional leaflets or other items dropped into periodicals or similar handy vehicles
style of house	set of rules used by printer or publisher in typesetting and make-up (see also 'house style')
stylus (computers)	slimmer, neater version of 'light pen' → used to input signals on 'digitizing pad' →
s/u	abbreviation for 'squared-up' →
sub-editor	one who assists an editor in preparing copy for printing
subject to correction	important qualification to an 'OK to print'
subscript	same as 'inferior numeral or figure' →
subsidiaries	see 'end-matter'
substance of . . . (abbr: s/o)	way of measuring paper by weight of ream of specified size; now superseded in UK by 'g/m^2' →

213

substrate in photography, material (eg: celluloid) used as carrier of sensitized emulsion; in printing, material (eg: paper, board) used to print on

subtractive colour mixing reproducing colour by mixing or superimposing inks, paints or dyes, as distinct from 'additive colour mixing' →; in effect, all applications of ink, etc, to surface such as white paper subtract (absorb) some portion of white light reflected from it:

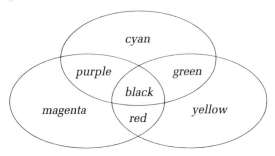

super-caster obsolescent 'hot metal' → Monotype machine for casting display size type, spaces, borders, leads, rules and ornaments

super ellipse one of range of regular, closed curves devised by Danish mathematician Piet Hein in 1959; best described as ellipse trying to turn into rectangle:

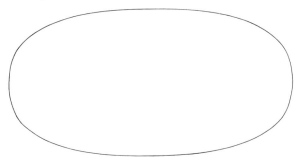

supercalendered paper glossy (but not coated) paper produced by being passed through 'supercalender' rolls under great pressure

superfiche 'microfiche' → having greater image reduction than standard and able to accommodate up to 400 'pages'

superior numeral / figure or letter small character set above level of normal characters of typeface (eg: $4^3 = 64$)

supers in cinefilm and TV, lettering or graphics superimposed on film

superscript same as 'superior numeral or letter' →

supershift one on keyboard of photocomposition machine giving access to another mode, such as change of typeface

surprinting	1) in photomechanical reproduction, combining two or more negatives to produce single new image; similar to 'stripping-up-as-one' → but with implication that extra negative stage may be involved (mainly US term) 2) US term for 'overprinting' →
swash character	one with emphatic flourish, thus:

ABDEFGHJ

(note that 'J' was originally swash form of 'I')

swatch	sample for colour, texture or pattern, whether for reproduction or one-off use
swell (of book)	extra bulking at back of book as result of sewing; reduced by 'smashing' in bookbinder's press
swelled dash/rule	one like this:

---

swept surface (computer graphics)	3D representation of symmetrical, curved object such as bottle, vase or glass, constructed by making line of half the profile and 'sweeping' it through 180 degrees:

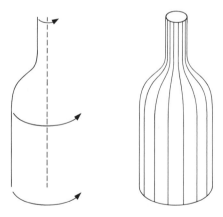

symbol	any figure devised and accepted as representation of some object, idea, activity, process, relationship or combination of these
sync-sound	in cinefilm and TV, synchronization of sound with images
synchronous (computers)	said of system having established time constant that controls transmission of 'bits' or 'characters'

215

synecdoche (pron: sineckdocky)	rhetorical figure in which whole represents a part, or part represents the whole (see also 'pars pro toto')
syntactics	see 'semiotics'
synthesis	building up separate elements into new, connected whole; see also 'analysis'

T

T (= time)	in photography, setting on camera shutter for use in making long exposures; when exposure release is pressed, shutter is opened and remains open until exposure release is pressed again
T square	ruler with cross piece at one end, used in conjunction with drawing board when drawing parallel lines
tab index	one in which divisions are indicated by projecting tabs on foredge:

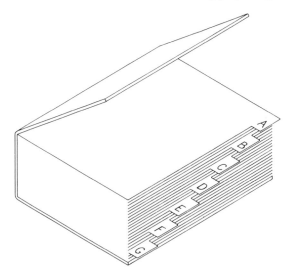

tabbing	1) arranging copy (typewritten or typeset) in multi-columnar pattern within set measure; colloquialism for 'tabulation' → 2) forming projecting portions to edges of book so as to make 'tab index' →
tablet (computers)	short for 'data tablet'; same as 'digitizing pad' → or 'bit pad'

tablet menu (computers)	'menu' → that is implanted in 'tablet' → rather than on screen
tabloid	newspaper format half the size of 'broadsheet newspaper' →
tabulation	arranging information in list, or table form
tachistoscope	optical instrument that reveals chosen image at measured brief intervals to allow observation of viewer response
tactile keyboard	one that does not contain raised keys but has gridded, touch-sensitive flat surface
tag (computers)	same as 'flag' →
tail	bottom of book →; also known as 'foot', especially in US
tail margin	see 'page'
take	1) portion of whole typesetting job allocated to one compositor 2) in cinefilm, single shooting of one scene
take back	instruction to printer on proof: take line or lines of type back to previous page or column
take in	instruction to printer on manuscript or proof to take in added copy
take over	instruction to printer on proof: take line or lines of type over to next column or subsequent page
taking lens	on twin lens camera, lens that throws image onto film, as distinct from viewing lens
tandem working	arranging print job so that two machines are combined to run in line
tape-driven (computers)	said of any system, such as photocomposition, that is activated by magnetic tape
tear sheet	file copy of editorial content or advertisement torn from periodical
tear test	tearing sheet of paper to discover direction of grain: will tear more cleanly in line of grain than across it
Tecdoc, tec doc (computers)	abbreviation for 'technical documentation': computer-controlled on-demand printing of catalogues, price lists, maintenance manuals and documents
tele-	prefix meaning 'at a distance'
telecommunication	sending or receiving signals, sounds or messages of any kind by television, radio, telegraph, telephone or other electromagnetic means

telecommuting	conducting business by use of computers and telecommunication links rather than travelling to offices in person
Telecopier	trade name for device that transmits graphic information over ordinary telephone line
Telefax	name of West German/French 'facsimile transmission' → service
Telefax 201	name of Netherlands 'facsimile transmission' → service
teleinformatics	body of techniques relating to data transfer by telecommunication channels; also known as 'telematics'
teleprinter	typewriter-like device using continuous stationery, used to communicate with similar device over 'telex' → link or as input to/output from computer; output is usually (though not necessarily) typewritten (see 'teletypewriter')
Teletel	name of public 'videotex' → service in France
teletex	sophisticated type of 'telex' → linking distant terminal with 'word-processor' →; *not* to be confused with 'teletext'
teletext	system employing some portion of broadcast television signal capacity to transmit text and graphics data in place, or as well as, analog picture data; alphanumerics closely resemble, or are identical to, 'videotex' → and both are referred to sometimes as 'videotext'
Teletypesetter (TTS)	trade name for device producing perforated tape for use in certain typecasting machines
teletypewriter	'teleprinter' → with typewritten input and output
telex	telegraphic system by which messages are sent from one teleprinter to another over public telephone network (term derived from *tele*-printer *ex*change)
Telidon	name of public 'videotex' → system in Canada
tertiary colour	one resulting from combination of two 'secondary colours' →
text/graphics merging (computers)	simultaneous drawing of information from storage medium containing text and one containing graphics program
text letter	yet another (confusing) synonym for 'black letter' →
text retrieval terminal (computers)	device that takes data from one computer to another; also known as 'milking machine' and 'fart box'
text type	any type that may be used for continuous text, up to 14pt
thermal printing	method using specially coated paper containing dyes that react to heat; dot matrix character elements are heated to correct temperature

	and impart image on contact without use of ink
Thermo-Fax	trade name for well-known make of thermocopy
thermocopy	one achieved by heat as against light (photocopy)
thermography	technique in which heat-treated ink image produces raised effect (note: not complete printing process)
thick (space)	commonly used word space in handsetting: ⅓ em of set
thimble printer	one having typewriter head similar in function to 'golf-ball' → but shaped like thimble
thin (space)	commonly used word space in handsetting: ⅕ em of set
thin-window	in 'photocomposition' → and 'word-processing' →, horizontal display area accommodating only one line of characters
third angle projjection	see 'multiview projections'
thirtytwo-mo, 32mo	cut or folded sheet that is one thirtysecond of a basic sheet size
thirtytwo-sheet poster	poster size 120 × 160in (3048 × 4065mm)
thorn	Old English/Old Norse character representing 'th' as in thorn:

$$þ$$

thread sealing	book binding technique whereby threads are pushed through sections, open ends of threads being glued along spine
threadless binding	same as 'perfect binding' → and 'unsewn binding'
three-colour process	similar to 'four-colour process' → except that there is no separate black printing; also called 'trichromatic system'
three-point perspective	see 'perspective projections'
throughput	production rate of any machine, calculated according to number of items passing through it; eg: throughput of photocomposition system could be quoted in 'characters per second' (cps)
throw-out	same as 'fold-out' →
throw up	instruction to printer to emphasize word, phrase, sentence or paragraph

thumb index	one in which thumb-sized chunks are cut out of foredge for greater ease of reference:

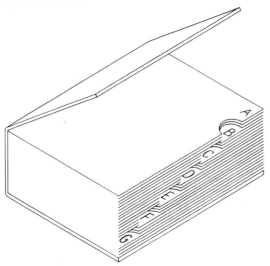

thumbnail	miniature sketch design or layout
thumbwheels (VDU)	mechanism in which vertical and horizontal movement on screen is controlled by manipulating pair of wheels set into keyboard:

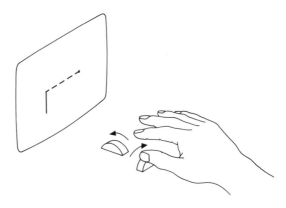

TicTac	name of French 'videotex' → system
tied letter	same as 'ligature' →
tilde	see 'accented (diacritical) signs'
time exposure	in photography, lengthy exposure of film – anything from few seconds to several hours – which may be for purpose of obtaining blurred movement or because light from subject is too weak

time-lapse photography	in cinefilm, method in which prolonged process, such as plant growth, is photographed in sequence of single exposures and then projected at normal speed
time sharing (computers)	system which accommodates itself to multiple use by switching at high speed to fulfil discrete portions of each user's input requirement in strict order
tint (of colour)	result of admixing small amounts of white with basic hue
tint laying	imparting ideas of tint to 'film assembly' → by means of 'stripping-in' →
tint plate	one used to print colour background to type, line or halftone matter
TIP TOP (computers)	acronym for *tape input/tape output*: system using magnetic tape for both input and output
tipping in/on	attaching single leaf to section of book or periodical by means of strip of paste or glue at back edge; see also 'guarding'
title page	that page of book carrying title, author and publisher
title sheet/section	first sheet or section of book, usually having no signature, so that second part is printed as 'B' or '2' signature, indicating that there is one preceding it
titling	'font/fount' → of capitals only, cast on body having very short 'beard' →, since there are no descenders
to view	part of phrase such as '8 pages to view' meaning eight pages imposed on one side of sheet that is 16 page 'section/signature' →
toenails	printer's slang for 'parentheses' →
toggle (computers)	any command that has function of switching an operation off if it is on, and on if it is off
tone separation	same as 'posterization' →
toners	in photography, chemicals used to convert black tones of bromide print into another colour, eg: sepia
tooling	synonym for 'blocking' →; term more common in US
topography	science of representing features of any district in detail, as on map
topology	branch of mathematics concerned with contiguity and relative position, rather than with congruence and dimension
touch panel (computers)	sensitive portion of 'touch sensitive screen' →

touch screen terminal
(computers)

same as 'touch sensitive screen' →

touch sensitive board/tablet
(computers)

input device that may perform (according to its construction) either as an alternative to 'keypad' → or simple 'digitizing pad' →

touch sensitive screen
(computers)

VDU that incorporates sensing device able to detect touch on screen as signal to activate some part of 'software' → program

TQ

initials of *t*ypographic *q*uality: said of computer-driven laser printer having degree of resolution suitable for setting text for conventional printed work

tracing materials

used for drawings of which direct reproduction copies are required; following types are available:
detail paper (cheap, not very translucent, tears easily);
natural tracing paper (cheap, translucent but tears easily);
prepared tracing paper (more expensive, more durable but less translucent);
tracing cloth (expensive, very durable, reasonably translucent but needs preparation before use);
acetate-based (expensive, very translucent but tears easily and becomes brittle);
polyester-based (very expensive, very translucent, very durable, dimensionally stable)

trackball
(computer graphics)

same as 'rolling-ball' →

tracking

in cinefilm and TV, movement of camera along track in relation to subject:

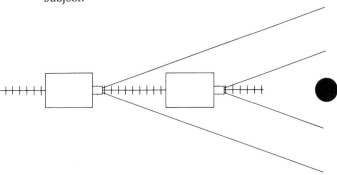

tracking

in lithography, making final correction to colour inking on machine by adjusting amount of ink along certain strips or tracks parallel to direction of sheet feed without affecting ink strength on other tracks

trade mark

word, words or graphic device intended to denote relationship between goods or services to which it is applied and proprietor of mark; in UK trade mark must be registered with Patent Office

trade setter	one who sets and proofs type for others and does not print in quantity
tranny	slang for 'transparency'
transaction (computers)	sequence of exchanges between operator and computer which involves some processing of these exchanges within the system, ie: entering on 'file' → of 'record' →
transfer lettering	image of type or other lettering which is transferred from transparent backing sheet by pressure; also called 'dry transfer'
transferring (lithography)	drawing or impressing inked image onto special coated paper and transferring it thence to lithographic printing surface
transitional	class of typefaces dating from mid-18th century, having somewhat finer serifs and hairlines than 'old-face' but not to extent of 'modern':

ABDE most pages

transparency	photographic image, usually coloured and positive, on transparent film; may be used either as basis for photomechanical reproduction, for backlit display or for slide projection
transparency viewer	in print production and processing, one specially made for this purpose with standard light source at 5000 Kv (Kelvins) for examining colour
travelling matte	see 'matte'
triangle	US term for 'set-square' →
triangular graph	one that is able to demonstrate three variables instead of only two:
trichromatic system	colour reproduction by three-colour, instead of four-colour, separation; same as 'three-colour process' →
trigram, trigraph	combination of three letters that represent one sound, as in 'eau' of b*eau*
trim marks	those incorporated on sheet when printed, to show how job is to be trimmed, and which are not visible in printed result
trimetric projection	see 'axonometric projections'
trimming	final cutting to size of printed job by guillotine
trs	abbreviation for 'transpose'; instructions on manuscript or proof to transpose character, word, phrase or sentence
TRT	initials of *t*ext *r*etrieval *t*erminal →

true small cap	type character intended for use as small cap, as distinct from one adapted for purpose, either by using cap from small type size or (in photocomposition) by photographic reduction from cap of same size
TTL meter	exposure meter situated within camera body, measuring light passing through lens (TTL = *through-the-lens*)
TTS	1) abbreviation for '*teletypesetter*' → 2) initials of *True-to-Scale*: trade name for limited quantity reproduction process using gelatin plate; especially suitable for architectural and engineering drawings when accuracy and stability are needed
TTY	abbreviation of '*teletype*'
tungsten film	colour film for use in artificial light emitting from tungsten bulbs
tungsten halogen lamp	photographic light source consisting of special form of tungsten lamp with trace of a halogen gas, smaller and brighter than conventional lamp; sometimes called 'quartz-iodine' lamp, though it may not contain either quartz or iodine
turn up (type)	to reverse a type feet uppermost, to indicate that required character is not yet available
turnaround document (computers)	one that is encoded via computer so that it can be returned after use by human; example is retail tag which can be read by retailer, buyer and stock control computer
turned commas	same as 'inverted commas' →
turned in	normal 'case bound book' → cover in which covering material is wrapped round edges, rather than being trimmed
turned-over cover	one with extended flaps on foredge, similar to 'book jacket' →
turnkey operation (computers)	provision by dealer of complete computer system: 'hardware' →, 'software' → and training of operator(s)
turtle (computers)	1) wheeled robot controlled by 'keypad' → 2) VDU image that can be moved on screen like 'cursor' →
tweaking (computer graphics)	technique in which operator manipulates input control to elongate selected item already on screen
twelve-mo, 12mo	cut or folded sheet that is one twelfth of basic sheet size
twin-lens reflex	see 'camera types'
twin-wire paper	that which is made from machine producing paper which has no 'wire-mark' and so is smooth on both sides
two colour machine	one that prints two colours on one side of sheet in one pass

two-point perspective	see 'perspective drawings'
two-revolution press	cylinder press → that revolves continuously (as distinct from 'stop-cylinder press') and makes two revolutions to each impression
two-up, three-up, etc.	two, three or more images of same subject, printing simultaneously on same side of sheet; combinations of single and multiple images are feasible
2½ D (computer graphics)	modification to 2D drawing system whereby objects represented are arranged to overlap one another
2/2; 2/1	in specification for print, shorthand for: 'two colours printing on both sides of sheet'; 'two colours one side, one colour on the other'
type	1) piece of metal of standard height having raised image of character or characters on its upper face, assembled with other pieces to form line which is printed by letterpress (relief) process:

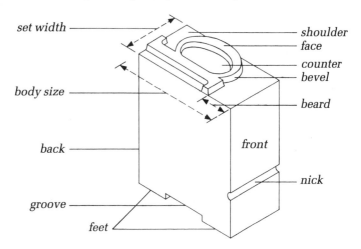

2) images obtained by printing from this metal
3) images obtained from composition systems which do not use metal type (eg: photocomposition)

type-ahead	said of electronic keyboard system that accepts text input or other commands whilst earlier keystrokes are still being executed
type area	specified area of page or trimmed sheet that contains body of text matter and illustrations (see 'page')
type family	all variants (eg: light, medium, bold, condensed, expanded) of all sizes of given type design
type-height	standard height of type from bed to printing surface in 'letterpress' → process: 0.918 inches in UK and US; also called 'height-to-paper'

type mark-up	typesetting instructions to compositor on manuscript or typescript, accompanied by general specification
type scale/gauge	rule marked in ems and points, and often also in inches and millimetres, for use in layout, imposition and proof correction; also called 'line gauge' and 'pica rule'
type series	those designs and sizes of typeface referred to by manufacturer by same series number
type specimen sheet	one giving full alphabets, figures and signs, with some text settings, of particular typeface
type-to-type	same as 'fold-to-print' →
typeface	printing surface of piece of type; by extension and more commonly, design of any particular set of types
typeface classification	several attempts have been made to evolve typeface classification systems, notably by Maximilien Vox in France (1954) and Deutscher Normenausschuss in Germany (1964); most recent is British Standard 2961: 1967 which is based on Vox system and lists classes of typefaces as follows:

humanist, formerly 'venetian' →
garalde, formerly 'old face' → or 'old style';
transitional →;
didone, formerly 'modern' →;
slab-serif →;
lineale, formerly 'sans-serif' → which divides into:
    grotesque;
    neo-grotesque;
    geometric;
humanist;
glyphic →;
script →;
graphic →;
and compounds of the above, eg: humanist/garalde

typewriter faces	there are two standard sizes: 'elite' (having twelve characters to the inch) and 'pica' (having ten characters to the inch), names also applied to the most common designs in these sizes:

```
This is a specimen of Elite type
```

```
This is a specimen of Pica type
```

typo	slang for 'typographic error'; can refer to either typewriting or typesetting mistake (US term)
typographer	confusing: in UK this term is often used to mean 'typographic designer' but in US it means 'one who sets type' (ie: compositor)

typography	originally (and still to some extent in US) art and technique of working with type; in UK it has come to mean, specifically, layout of typeset and accompanying graphic matter for reproduction
Typositor	trade name for make of photolettering machine

U

UCR	initials of 'undercolour removal' →
UDC	initials of 'Universal Decimal Classification': system of classifying areas of knowledge developed as extension of 'Dewey Decimal Classification' →
UDK (computers)	initials of 'user-defined key' →
Ultimatt	trade name for version of 'colour separation overlay' → system used by UK Independent Television News
ultra-violet	near-visible waves in 'electromagnetic spectrum' → which can affect some photographic materials and which may need to be absorbed by filters so as to reduce haze
ultrafiche	'microfiche' → composed of such minute images that 3,000 of them can be incorporated on one 4in × 6in fiche
umlaut	see 'accented (diacritical) signs'
undercolour removal	technique of reducing strength of colour in 'colour separations' → so as to economize on ink and / or facilitate overprinting of colours; abbreviated as UCR
underlay	in printing, same as 'interlay' →
unit system	in machine composition of type, method of relating character widths to unit measurements, originally developed by Monotype; units are not standard dimensions but vary according to 'set' →
Universal Copyright Convention 1952	agreement between signatory countries giving protection for copyright proprietor of text, photograph, illustration, movie, work of art, etc, providing work carries proper copyright notice consisting of © symbol, name of coyright proprietor and year of publication; both US and UK adhere to this convention
universal developer	in photography, one that can be used either for film or print development, depending on strength of solution

Unix (computers)	widely used operating system for 'minicomputers' devised in US by Bell Laboratories
unjustified on right / left	taken to mean type lines that line up horizontally on one side and are ragged on other; strictly speaking, all lines of type are 'justified' → but this misnomer is now hallowed by use; also described as 'quad left / right' or (preferably) 'ragged right / left' →
unjustified tape	in photocomposition, tape output of 'non-counting keyboard' in which operator makes no end-of-line decisions about justification and word-breaks; also called 'idiot tape'
un-shift	in photocomposition and word processing, un-happy synonym for 'lower case' →
unsewn binding	same as 'perfect binding' → and 'threadless binding'
up	of computer, one that is in operating condition, as against 'down'
UPC	initials of 'Universal Product Code' (see 'bar code')
update (computers)	add to, delete from or otherwise amend 'record' in data 'file' so as to bring it up to date
u/lc, U&LC	abbreviations for 'upper-and-lower-case'
u/v, U/V	initials of 'ultra-violet' →
upper-case	another name for 'capitals' → deriving from traditional position of that case containing capital letters, small caps and figures; most often used in expression 'upper-and-lower-case', meaning upper-case for initial letters of sentences and proper names, lower-case for rest
uprating film	in photography, exposing film at speed and stop applicable to higher 'ASA' → or 'DIN' rating, then giving it increased development to compensate for under-exposure; useful technique where lighting conditions are very poor
upstroke (of type)	lighter stroke in type character, deriving from upward movement of pen in calligraphy:

US Customary System	system of units of measurement, using inches and feet, pints and gallons, ounces and pounds; derived from, though not in all respects identical to, British Imperial System
useful redundancy	see 'redundancy'

user-defined key (computers)	one whose function may be defined by user to perform special command or sequence of commands
user-friendly (computers)	said of service, system, device or tool designed for greatest convenience, comfort and general satisfaction of user; one that incorporates full consideration of 'human factors studies' →
USIA	initials of *U*nited *S*tates *I*nformation *A*gency

V

vacuum forming	shaping thin plastic sheeting by means of vacuum:

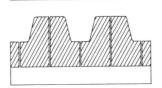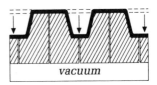

vacuum (printing) frame	illuminated printing frame used to make process negatives and positives; vacuum provides best contact between surfaces
vacuum packing	wrapping product in sealed plastic skin from which as much air as possible has been exhausted
value (of colour)	degree of lightness or darkness of colour in relation to neutral grey scale
Van Dyke print	photocopy in dark brown colour, used as proof; also known as 'brownprint'
vanishing point (abbr: VP)	in 'perspective projections' →, point at which all parallel lines which are also parallel to ground plane converge on horizon
vapour diazo	same as 'ammonia duplication process' →
variable space	said of those spaces between words in lines of type that are varied in width from line to line so as to even lines up
Varityper	trade name for make of typewriter specially designed for 'direct impression' → type composition
varnish	transparent liquid that can be added to ink or overprinted to give high-gloss finish
VDT	initials of 'visual display terminal' device incorporating keyboard, logic system and cathode ray tube (CRT), and connected to com-

puter; used to display alphanumeric or graphic information stored in computer, also to key in queries so that result of interrogation may be viewed on screen

VDU initials of 'visual *d*isplay *u*nit', cathode ray tube (CRT) may be used as part of 'VDT' → or as 'stand-alone' information device but now taken as virtually synonymous with VDT

vector generally, any quantity having both magnitude and direction and expressed by straight line of given length

vector diagram see 'star graph'

vector display
(computer graphics) presentation of data on VDU in which 'vectors' → are used to connect selected points, as for type representation:

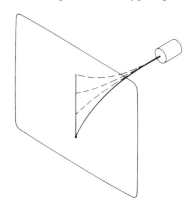

vehicle (of ink) carrier of ink pigment, all or mostly composed of varnish and solvent

vellum fine 'parchment' → made from inner side of calfskin

vellum finish smooth finish applied to paper

velox halftone-screened photoprint of continuous-tone subject, suitable for inclusion on camera-ready artwork along with line copy

venetian (of typeface) early form of roman that retains sloping bar to 'e' from calligraphic origin and has less variation between thick and thin strokes:

PAST the

Venn diagram one using circles, ovals or other closed figures to illustrate sets, named after John Venn, who used them from 1880; also known as 'Euler circles' after Leonhard Euler, who used them in 1770 (though they appear to have been invented by Johann Christoph Sturm in 1661):

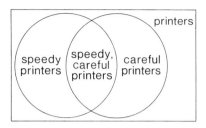

verso   any left-hand page of book; one which is even-numbered

vertex (pl: vertices)   in geometry, meeting-point of lines that form an angle

vertical raster count   total number of vertical divisions in 'raster' →

vertical scrolling   most common orientation of 'scrolling' →

vertical shift   same as 'rising front' →

VET   initials of 'visual editing terminal'; visual display terminal with specific editing function

VHS   initials of 'Video Home System, video cassette system developed by JVC

VHSIC (computers)   initials of very high speed integrated circuit

vide   Latin for 'see'; used in footnotes to direct reader to particular book, chapter or passage

video colorizer   system devised to convert monochrome original into full colour
(computer graphics)   electronic image, whether for video tape/disk, broadcast television or printed publication

video disk   device, usually of plastic, incorporating recorded visual and sound data for playback via television screen, as alternative to more usual 'video cassette recorder' (VCR) →; may be contact or non-contact (optical) type

video editor   in photocomposition, editing device incorporating 'CRT' →

video layout system   CRT system used for layout planning prior to photocomposition (see also 'area composition'); abbreviated as 'VLS'

video monitor   in videotape recording (VTR), device for viewing recording, at moment of shooting or afterwards when editing; like TV receiver without tuning controls

231

videomatics jargon for combination of video and information technologies

videotape magnetic recording tape used in recording TV signals, both sound and vision

videotex (computers) internationally accepted system devised to display computer-stored text and graphics via standard telephone lines, using video monitor or suitably equipped television set; also known (though less widely) as 'Viewdata'

Viditel name of Netherlands' 'videotex' → system

view camera one having ground glass screen at back for viewing and focusing at image plane

view volume (computer graphics) notional space in which constructed objects are said to exist in 3D display, based on x, y, z coordinate system:

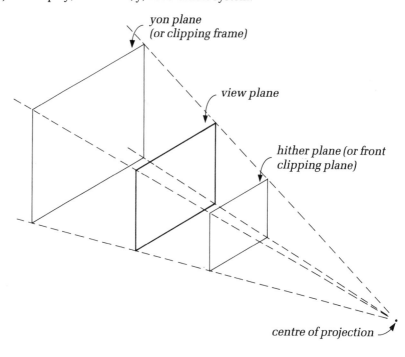

Viewdata UK Post Office trade name for what is more widely known as 'videotex' →

viewport (computers) preferred term for rectangular portion of VDU screen most frequently used to examine detail of previously displayed information, or to show clock or other instrumental array; also, though less accurately, known as 'window'

vignetted halftone	one in which edges are gradually shaded off into background:

virgule	same as 'oblique stroke', 'slash' or 'solidus' → (but notice that in French it means 'comma')
virtual scrolling (computers)	same as 'infinite scrolling' →
viscosity	stickiness: important characteristic in printing inks
Vista	name of Bell Canada's 'videotex' → system
visual	a representation to show intended result of print job; may be a quick sketch or 'presentation visual' →
visual display terminal	see 'VDT'
visual editing terminal	see 'VET'
visualizer	illuminated device that produces enlarged or reduced image for use in visual; may also be used as simple photoprinting enlarger
viz	abbreviation of *videlicet*, Latin for 'namely', used in footnotes
VLS	initials of 'video layout system' →
VLSI (computers)	initials of very large scale integration
volatile memory (computers)	one which loses its data if power supply is switched off, so beware!
volume	published work that, although separately bound, forms part of a larger whole
volume element	see 'voxel'
voucher copy	free copy of periodical given to advertiser who has an insertion in that issue

233

voxel (computer graphics)	short for 'volume element'; term used in some 3D imaging systems to represent solid 'picture element' →
VP	initials of '*v*anishing *p*oint' →
VTR	initials of '*v*ideo *t*ape *r*ecorder'

W

wallet envelope	one with quadrilateral, as distinct from, triangular, flap:

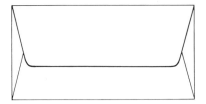

wallet-fold	same as 'gate-fold' (see 'folding methods') but may be applied more particularly to wallet-fold cover
wally box	slang for 'protocol converter' →
wash up	in printing, cleaning of rollers, ink ducts and press before another colour can be printed
watermark	faint design imparted into certain uncoated papers when they are being made, to identify mills they come from
web	reel or ribbon of paper as formed on paper-making machine
web-fed	used of printing machine in which paper is fed from web or reel rather than from flat sheets
web-offset	offset-litho printing machine that is 'web-fed' →
wedge-serif	typeface with triangular serifs, also known as 'latin':

ABCDEFabcdefg

weight (of type-face)	comparative strength of appearance of any typeface
wet-on-wet	printing technique in which one colour is printed on another whilst first one is still wet

wf	abbreviation of '*w*rong *f*ont/fount': correction to proof indicating that character from another typeface has been used in error
wheel graph	see 'pie graph'
white line	in typesetting, space between lines of type equal to that left if one line of type is omitted
white out	paint out anything on artwork that is not to be reproduced
white space	those areas of printed item not occupied by type matter or illustration, particularly those other than margins
white space skid	time-saving feature in some 'facsimile transmitters' → whereby scanner skips over white areas on document being transmitted
whole bound	same as 'full bound' →
widow	last line of typeset paragraph consisting of one word only; may be used by some to apply specifically to one coming on first line of new column
wild cel	in film animation, one not fixed to register pegs and thus able to move about freely under rostrum camera
wild track	in cinefilm, sound recorded without matching camera shot
WIMP (computer graphics)	acronym for *W*indow/*M*ouse/*P*ulldown menu: user-friendly interface system linking carefully matched input/output devices
Winchester disk (computers)	'magnetic disk' → that is in fact group of rigid disks revolving in vacuum; has greater storage capacity than orthodox disks
window	1) in photolitho processing, hole cut in 'flat' → for insertion of negative material which is to print down on plate 2) in typesetting, another word for 'river' →
window (computers)	same as 'viewport' →
window-to-viewport mapping (computer graphics)	activity of converting 'primitives' → from 'world coordinate system' → to 'device coordinate' → system
wipe	in cinefilm and TV editing, one shot moving in from side, top or bottom as viewed, progressively replacing previous shot
wipe on plate	litho plate that is sensitized manually just before image is printed down, as compared to 'pre-sensitized plate' →
wire-frame picture (computer graphics)	representation of three-dimensional object on VDU or graph plotter by outline drawing (see also 'hidden-edge removal')
wire-photo	technique of transmitting photograph (or any other pictorial form) by

means of photo-electric cells; also called 'phototelegraphy'

wire-side   that side of some uncoated papers (such as 'antiques') which shows a 'wire-mark', as distinct from 'felt-side'

wire-stitch/stab   to secure book by forcing wire through back of insetted work or side of gathered work

woodcut   relief printing block in which non-printing portions are cut away by knife along grain of wood, giving strong, simple black line:

wood-engraving   relief printed block similar to woodcut except that special engraving tools are used, cutting on end grain of wood to achieve finer effect:

woodfree (UK)   paper that is free of mechanical wood pulp, using chemical pulp instead; known in US as 'freesheet'

word-breaking   splitting words at end of line of type to avoid gappy wordspacing and 'rivers' →

word processor   computer designed for inputting, editing and storing text on magnetic tape or disk; is commonly used as front end for 'daisy-wheel' → or 'laser printer' →, and may also provide input for photocomposition system

word spacing   in machine composition other than linecasting, word spacing conforms to 'unit system' →; in hand composition, word spaces are provided in the following widths:

em quad   *en quad*   *thick*   *middle*   *thin*

word wraparound,
wordwrap
(computers)

in word-processing and photocomposition, correction procedure whereby VDU display drops down a line to accommodate newly amended item in text; following this, remainder of subsequent text is adjusted to fit up to any change in length

work and back

same as 'sheetwise' →; rarely used

work and turn

to print 'forme' → on one side of sheet, turn it over from left to right and print same forme on reverse, thus producing two identical half-sheets; most common type of 'half-sheet work' (see appendix):

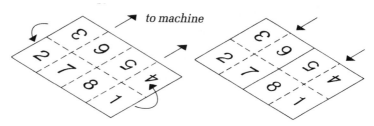

work and tumble

similar to 'work and turn', except that sheet is turned over from 'gripper edge' → to back, instead of from left to right (see appendix):

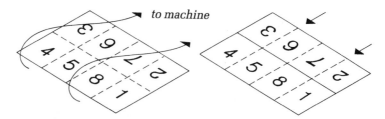

work and twist

to print forme on one side of sheet, then turn it round (not over) and print again from same forme (particularly suited to work involving crossed rules):

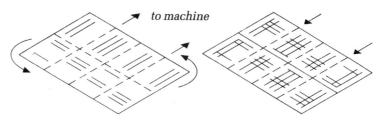

work print	in cinefilm, same as 'cutting copy' →; more common in US
work up	in letterpress, type space which has been accidentally pushed up
working	in printing, one operation on printing machine, whether of inking, stamping, creasing, perforating or embossing
world coordinate space (computer graphics)	system whereby 3D object is defined using coordinates, thus allowing it to be called up on screen
WORM	acronym for *write once read many*: 'optical digital disk' – on which data recorded may not be erased
wove paper	uncoated paper that has an even, unpatterned look-through
wrap-around plate	letterpress plate that wraps around cylinder, similar to offset-litho plate
wrap-around press	letterpress machine using curved printing plate wrapped around cylinder
wrap-around, wrap-round	small printing section (4pp or 8pp) wrapped around another section in gathered work (see 'gathering'; also known as 'outset')
wrapped surface (computer graphics)	same as 'swept surface' →
wrapper	see 'book jacket'
wrappering cover	attaching cover to paperback book or periodical by glueing to spine only (see also 'drawing-on cover')
wraps and inserts	said of those sections of book in different paper to main text (typically to incorporate specially printed illustrations) which are either 'wrap-round' → or inserted into centre of standard section/signature
writing (as noun)	smooth-surfaced paper suitable for stationery
wrong fount/font (wf)	correction mark indicating that character from one fount/font has strayed into matter typeset in another one
wrong grain direction	said of paper used in book production where 'grain direction' → runs across page rather than down, thus putting strain on spine
wrong-reading	see 'reverse reading'
wyn	obsolete Middle English character representing 'w' as in 'wet':

$$\text{\Large{þ}}$$

WYSIWYG acronym for *w*hat *y*ou *s*ee *i*s *w*hat *y*ou *g*et: aphorism describing relationship between, for example, VDU display and final output in photocomposition system

X

x-axis horizontal axis in 'coordinate graph' →

x-height mean height of lower case type characters which have neither ascenders nor descenders:

x-ref abbreviation for 'cross-reference'

xerography printing process in which image is projected onto plate, causing electrostatic charge already imparted to be discharged where light falls, thus allowing applied coating of resinous powder to adhere only to uncharged areas and then transfer to paper; also known as 'photostatic' or 'dry copying' process:

surface is electrostatically charged

image projected onto surface dissipates charge in illuminated areas

applied 'toner' powder adheres to areas which retain charge and is then fixed by heat

x–y plotter same as 'graph plotter' →
(computers)

xylography posh name for wood-block printing

239

yapp binding binding form in which limp cover overlaps leaves of book (after William Yapp, who devised it for his pocket bibles)

y-axis vertical axis in 'coordinate graph' →

yon plane notional back plane in 'view volume' →, as compared to 'hither
(computer graphics) plane' →

z-axis one indicating depth in 3D coordinate system:

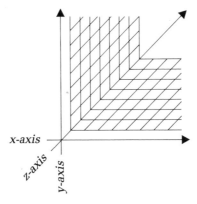

z-dipping limiting notional space in 3D system by defining 'hither plane' → and
(computer graphics) 'yon plane' → in 'view volume' →

zenithal projections group of projections of Earth in which plane of projection is assumed to touch globe at single point, as distinct from 'cylindrical' → or 'conic' → projections; typical zenithal projections are:

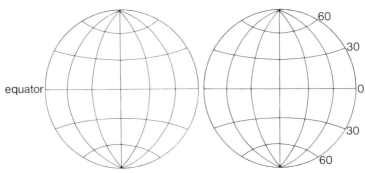

Lambert's equatorial zenithal equal area

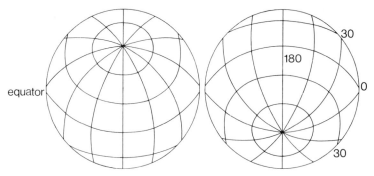

Lambert's oblique zenithal equal area

zig-zag book one made as continuous, concertina fold, usually printed one side only; may be stitched at back or left unstitched so that it may be opened up, either for display or to reveal printed reverse:

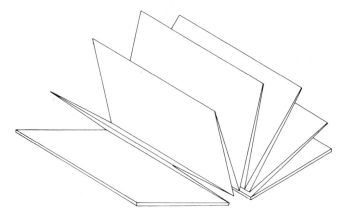

bibliophiles call zig-zag book formed from manuscript roll an 'orihon'

zinco, zincograph letterpress line plate made of zinc

Zöllner's lines well-known optical illusion in which parallel lines are made to appear to diverge by means of oblique lines intersecting them:

zoom lens variable-focus camera lens; way of having several lenses in one

zooming in cinefilm and TV, using zoom lens to decrease or increase 'field area' → during shooting, so that camera appears to approach or

241

retreat from subject (see also 'tracking'):

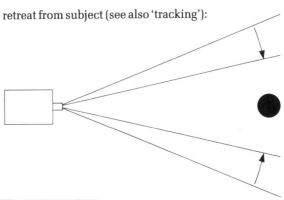

effect of 'zooming-in'

effect of 'tracking-in' for comparison

appendix: some typical backed-up imposition plans

expansion of entry given under 'imposition' → providing instant
check for backing-up of 8pp, 12pp and 16pp 'section' →; following
pages show alternatives to 'sheetwise' → impositions for 'half-sheet
work'

machine direction → → →

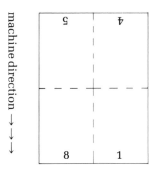

side A of 8pp imposition (backing side B overleaf)

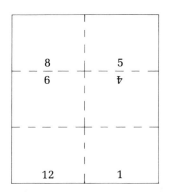

side A of 12pp imposition (backing side B overleaf)

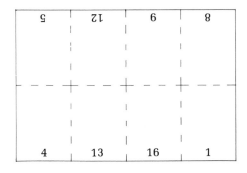

side A of 16pp imposition (backing side B overleaf)

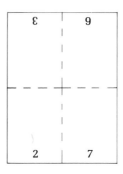

side B of 8pp imposition (backing side A overleaf)

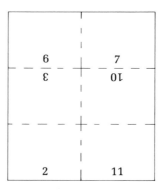

side B of 12pp imposition (backing side A overleaf)

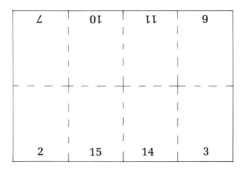

side B of 16pp imposition (backing side A overleaf)

244

some typical work-and-turn imposition plans

expansion of entries given under 'imposition' → and 'work-and-turn' →, showing 'half-sheet work' alternative to 'sheetwise' impositions

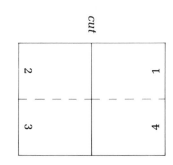

8pp work-and-turn imposition (see also overleaf)

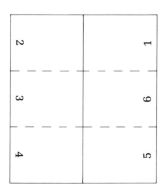

12pp work-and-turn imposition (see also overleaf)

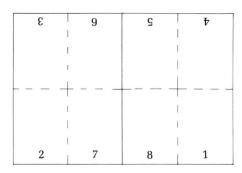

16pp work-and-turn imposition (see also overleaf)

some typical work-and-turn impositions *continued*

plans shown below are identical to those overleaf, but reversed side-to-side so as to provide two identical half-sheets; thus 8pp work-and-turn imposition gives two 4pp sections (signatures), 12pp work-and-turn gives two 6pp leaflets, and 16pp work-and-turn gives two 8pp sections (signatures)

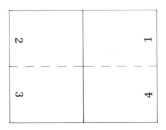

8pp work-and-turn imposition (see also overleaf)

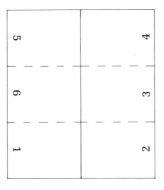

12pp work-and-turn imposition (see also overleaf)

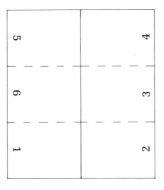

16pp work-and-turn imposition (see also overleaf)

some typical work-and-tumble imposition plans

expansion of entries given under 'imposition' → and 'work-and-tumble' →, showing 'half-sheet work' alternative to 'sheetwise' impositions

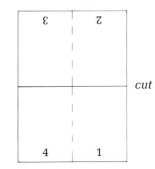

8pp work-and-tumble imposition (see also overleaf)

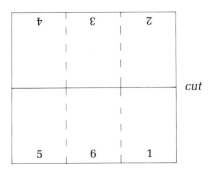

12pp work-and-tumble imposition (see also overleaf)

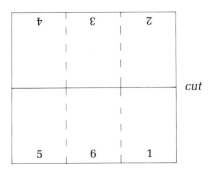

16pp work-and-tumble imposition (see also overleaf)

247

some typical work-and-tumble impositions *continued*

plans below are identical to those overleaf, but reversed head to foot so as to provide two identical half-sheets; thus 8pp work-and-tumble imposition gives two 4pp sections (signatures), 12pp work-and-tumble gives two 6pp leaflets, and 16pp work-and-tumble gives two 8pp leaflets

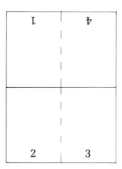

8pp work-and-tumble imposition (see also overleaf)

12pp work-and-tumble imposition (see also overleaf)

16pp work-and-tumble imposition (see also overleaf)